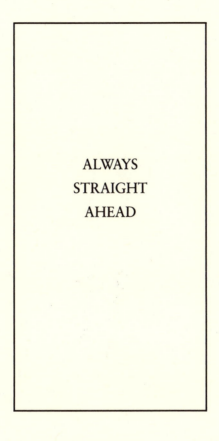

ALWAYS
STRAIGHT
AHEAD

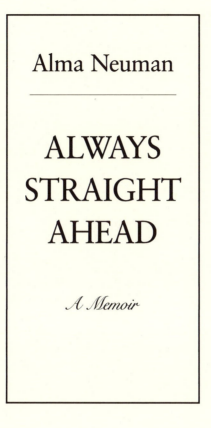

Alma Neuman

ALWAYS
STRAIGHT
AHEAD

A Memoir

LOUISIANA STATE UNIVERSITY PRESS
Baton Rouge and London

Copyright © 1993 by Joel Agee
All rights reserved
Manufactured in the United States of America
First printing
02 01 00 99 98 97 96 95 94 93   5 4 3 2 1

Designer: Glynnis Phoebe
Typeface: Sabon / Snell Roundhand
Typesetter: G & S Typesetters, Inc.
Printer and binder: Thomson-Shore, Inc.

Library of Congress Cataloging-in-Publication Data

Neuman, Alma, 1912–1988.
    Always straight ahead : a memoir / Alma Neuman.
      p. cm.
    ISBN 0-8071-1792-7 (cloth)
      1. Neuman, Alma, 1912–1988—Family.   2. Women sculptors—United
States—Biography.   3. Intellectuals—United States—Biography.
4. Agee, James, 1909–1955—Marriage.   5. Uhse, Bodo, 1904–1963—
Marriage.   6. Neuman, Alma, 1912–1988—Homes and haunts—Mexico.
7. Neuman, Alma, 1912–1988—Homes and haunts—Germany.   I. Title.
CT275.N458A3   1993
730'.92—dc20
[B]   92-20844
                                                                                  CIP

Some of the material in this book appeared in slightly different form in "Thoughts of
Jim: A Memoir of Frenchtown and James Agee," *Shenandoah*, XXXIII (1983).

The paper in this book meets the guidelines for permanence and durability of the
Committee on Production Guidelines for Book Longevity of the Council on Library
Resources. ∞

Contents

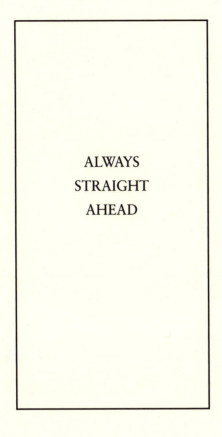

ALWAYS
STRAIGHT
AHEAD

Introduction

I would not have thought of writing about myself were it not for a letter from James Agee, my first husband, which I received twenty-five years after it was written. The letter arrived by airmail from England some twenty years after his death. It was sent by a stranger, who enclosed a note of explanation: he had found the letter among Agee's manuscripts shortly after Jim's death, realized it was meant for me, pocketed it, misplaced it, then found it again years later and sent it on. The note, deeply apologetic, also warned me to be prepared for what the sender called an "emotional shock." In wonder, I started to read the long letter enclosed, recognizing instantly Jim's minuscule handwriting. I did not take the warning seriously—too much had happened in the many years since Jim's death. My third husband, Bill, had died suddenly, and, just five months before, my beloved son Stefan had finally ended his own life's pain, all scarcely a year before the letter arrived. I did not believe anything in a letter written so long ago could touch me. I was wrong. Here, then, is the letter:

March 20, 1953

Alma darling—
  Just now I'll propose all the reasons why I'm writing you at just this time. To hell with them. But all right, for two: I've just sent a cable to [our

son] Joel, giving my new address, and hoping I'll hear from you. And the other: Helen [Levitt] just tonight gave me a photograph she made during our summer on the farm near Stockton—and seeing it, I—fourteen years dropped out from under me, and I knew just where we were then, and where we really belong, and where we always ought to be.

I am still in love with you, Alma. This is different from adding "I always will be." I don't know or care whether I always will be—but I know I still am—and after all this time, and all the things between, that means a terrible amount to me. Whether it means that I would break up my life with Mia and two children (any more than you might with Bodo and Joel and Stefan) I don't know. I at least have learned, since I last knew you, that life can get too thick to solve. But I do know, that that question, is as powerful in my life, as anything I know: whether you and I can ever live again as man and woman.

Now for a minute forget caution and good manners, and I will also forget however you may feel, and only tell about myself.

Alma—I have two children. I love them both, very dearly. I also love their mother, very dearly. Since knowing you, I have also fallen in love, once, very hard, with an Irish girl who possibly moved me even more, sexually, than you did. But the more I know of everything, the more I know what a hopeless slut she is, compared with you—and also how hopeless my life is, compared with life with you. I gave the Irish girl up, for the sake of everything I feel about Mia and our children. I at least believe I might give everything else up, to be with you again. I said, a minute back, that life is too thick to solve. Maybe it is. But is it? Alma, can we bring our lives back together?

God knows where you may be, in relation to memory, but I know where I am. Any amount that is dear to me, is since I knew you. But all the roots of all I care most for, go back to you. I know you were my natural wife, forever—and I believe I was your natural husband. And seeing this half-second snapshot, out of fifteen years ago, in our car, waiting for the train, I knew it again, instantaneously. Just seeing your face, I knew both things: "I love this girl" and "you are my wife"—and "we should have so many children."

Oh, come back to me, my beloved.

Alma, baby, dearest, love, dear wife—I'm writing blind. I won't send this, or any addition, unless I hear from the cable I sent Joel tonight—because I won't know where to, for one thing.

I'm writing blind in other ways. I can assume you are at least as deeply absorbed in your life as I am in mine. And I have no faith in what words can do, against proximity. So, I have wished so much, that I could get to Europe, and see you, and Joel. Over and over, I've written you as I feel now, and never sent it. And another reason I haven't is, I so like and respect Bodo, and recognize so deeply, your life together. So all I do ask is, that you *consider* what I write you now, rather than throwing it immediately away. I owe very great debts, by now, to another person. So do you. But are these debts absolute? Shouldn't we at least think about it and talk about it?

I would be tempted instead to say: come back—or let me come over—let us get to know what we most care about again—before too late. For one thing, I am 43, and you are 40—if we should (as I believe), we should have as many children as possible, while we can.

All right. The pitch about Mia? I love and revere her, as I believe you do Bodo. But she never replaced you, with me. The nearest I ever came to a girl who did, was the Irish girl I spoke of. There, the sexual love was extreme. But I have left her for Mia. And in all retrospect, I know how much more I love you, than her, or Mia, or anyone—

Think of our coming back together, is all I can say. I know that even once we think of it we should meet, in leisure if possible, and try to find out for sure in the present—but if we do that, I feel sure we will come back—

I wonder whether I'll ever send this to you. I certainly won't, unless I hear an address from you—

Jim

I love you Alma. I love you Alma.

Before the end of the first page, I was wandering around my apartment from room to room, saying Jim's name over and over. Then I sat down in the living room and read it through to the end, mostly crying—wanting so badly to answer it. The frustration and need to answer were finally eased by the thought, Why not? I'll write Jim anyway and tell all about my life since he died. And I actually did start a "Dearest Jim" letter. It didn't work, there was too much. Friends then urged me to tell of my life, nevertheless, since Jim Agee did, after all, represent just a part of a story which, I came to believe, should be told—as completely and truthfully as it is possible to tell of oneself.

1 *The Hill*

$\mathcal{I}$ was sixteen when I started going up to "the Hill." The Hill was Hamilton College; it was the Saunders family, and the elegant nineteenth-century house on the campus which was their home; and (sometime later) it was Frisk, the Saunders boy with whom I was in love.

Frisk first approached me one day after school. "Will you be doing anything this Saturday?" (The *t* in *Saturday* was clipped and clear, not "saddurdy" as I was used to hearing and saying it.) "I'll have to ask my mother," I said. And so it was that my mother called Mrs. Saunders and arrangements were made for me to spend the college house-party weekend on the Hill. Frisk, as a professor's son, had the privilege of inviting a girl, even though, at scarcely seventeen, he was not yet in college. For me, it would be my first weekend away from home—and the first "date" I took seriously.

Strange that out of that entire weekend all I can remember is a pincushion. It stood on the dresser in the room where I was to rest that first afternoon until called for dinner. The pincushion, replete with pins, needles, and various colored threads, represented for me an uncommon thoughtfulness and nicety I was not used to, and a world I longed to be a part of.

Whatever may have occurred that weekend, I must have done and said the right things, because Frisk and I began to see each other more and more, and I became a frequent guest. I spent almost as much time on the Hill as I did with my own family in Utica, just ten miles away in northern New York.

I can still see them all clearly: Olivia, whom everyone called Via, the younger daughter, some eight years older than I—poised, witty, educated, and since I was none of these things, inaccessible. Silvia, the oldest—fresh-faced, cheerful and handsome, also witty, college educated and equally inaccessible. The boy was never called Percy, or Blake, his given names—he was Frisk to everyone.

It was soon evident, not only to Frisk and me, but to those around us, that we were in love. I believe it was that fact that represented, certainly at first, what can only be called my "in" with the Saunders family. I did not seek an "in," but I was aware that being accepted and invited there was an enviable and sought-after distinction. Guests of the Saunderses had, invariably, two attributes: good family lineage and some outstanding artistic talent. So it helped that I played the violin and was, in fact, an accomplished musician, already playing Mozart concertos and Bach sonatas: it would, I hoped, balance out the regrettable circumstance that I was Jewish and that my father was a businessman and uneducated. Ashamed as I was of both these facts, I clung with a kind of desperation to thoughts of my mother's superiority, her good looks and cultural aspirations. I suspect my own prettiness helped to overcome a heavy sense of inferiority and inadequacy which almost always surfaced in the presence of the Saunderses, and which was surely the cause of the utterly unnatural role I sensed was called for: an instinctive shaping of myself to represent, as nearly as possible, the girl they either thought I was or wanted me to be. And so I did a good deal of role playing. I rarely felt the enthusiasm I often expressed, and the craving for culture and knowledge I sometimes displayed was more pretended than real. Once the act was begun, of course, it was impossible to undo with any grace. So it was not unusual to find myself in painful predicaments. I remember in particular one icy winter night when I stood on the campus lawn while Dr. Saunders explained and pointed out the constellations which I could see through his large and efficient telescope. I know I witnessed the ring around Saturn, but what I mainly remember is how miserably cold I was. Dr. Saunders knew me to be avid for knowledge, and I couldn't let him down. So I stood, staunch under a cold moon, trembling with cold, my face aglow with interest and appreciation, all the while longing for the end of the lesson, and a quick walk back to the house and the warmth of the music room's fireplace.

Yet I almost literally adored Dr. Saunders, and even now, with the perspective of over fifty years, I think of him as deserving in most part the admiration, respect, and even love that almost everyone seemed to have for him. Dr. Saunders was professor of chemistry at the college, but I think his main love and interests were for music and horticulture. I can still see him coming into the house from the Ribbon, a narrow strip of land a short distance from the campus house, where he grew and hybridized rare peonies. His sleeves are carelessly rolled back almost to the elbows, showing strong forearms and hands caked with drying earth. He calls out a friendly greeting to whoever might be around for lunch as he makes his way upstairs to wash up. Dr. Saunders—handsome, bearded, charming Dr. Saunders who taught me so much, but especially how to play the viola. Once I had learned the viola clef, our only difficulty in arranging for string quartets lay in finding a cellist. Dr. Saunders eventually hired one for us. Frisk could manage second violin; Dr. Saunders could then relinquish the viola parts to me and play first violin. I think he knew most of the chamber-music literature by heart, besides which he seemed to be able to sight-read practically anything. We practiced and played string quartets for hours at a time, for weeks, months—one whole summer we worked on the Opus 132 of Beethoven, with the Haydn and Mozart quartets in between. Dr. Saunders and I played at every opportunity, and when Frisk was away or not at hand, we got another second violinist, usually more capable, and my vacations from Skidmore were spent mostly on the Hill playing string quartets.

Our playing was mostly for our own pleasure and rarely for an audience, though I remember one afternoon playing a Mozart quartet and realizing that Alexander Woolcott was sitting in one of the wicker chairs in the music room. Woolcott, an alumnus of the college and a good friend of the Saunderses', neither expected nor wanted to be entertained, since he was himself an entertainer, a wit; he liked to talk and hold court, so to have to watch and listen to the four of us, engrossed in our playing and oblivious to his presence, must have been a dreary experience for him.

Sometimes there were live-in students, usually the children of wealthy friends. I can recall now only the Grant girls, great-granddaughters of Ulysses S. Grant, whose parents paid Dr. and Mrs. Saunders for tutoring as well as the cultural and scholastic atmosphere their house provided.

Mrs. Saunders was a supremely cultivated woman somewhere in her fifties, with sharp eyes and the softly beaked nose of an aristocrat. Her almost voracious ambition for me, her amazing tenacity and fierce energy were sometimes hard to escape, though she was always kind to me. Still, I rarely felt at ease with her. Mrs. Saunders' sister, Aunt Mathilda, who occasionally came to visit, was another matter—I knew her instinctively as my enemy. To Aunt Mathilda, breeding and family lineage was everything. She despised Jews, and somehow I knew without knowing that she feared that Frisk and I might someday marry, that bad blood might come into the family. So, if behind Mrs. Saunders' drive to cultivate and educate me there was, quite probably, the need to make me, as far as possible, suitable in spite of my background, I also knew that Aunt Mathilda was pressuring not only her sister, but her nephew Frisk as well, to seek out more suitable blood. But meanwhile, and especially during the year and a half before I went away to Skidmore, Frisk and I were in love, and I continued to spend most of my time with the Family.

Mrs. Saunders in particular saw to it that I was present when someone of importance was visiting, during after-concert receptions, or when anything special was going on. And something was often going on, with people milling about in the music room to meet the Guest or Guests. Then Mrs. Saunders, kind and gracious as always, would introduce me, always using a descriptive label: "I want you to meet Alma—she's our violist—such a fine musician—she and my husband play string quartets together." Actually, such an introduction did supply me with a much-needed justification for being there.

Of course, I felt more inadequate than I actually was. For I was not only a good musician, but was never again to know as much about music as I did during those years. I remember Dr. Saunders standing before the record player, and the rest of us, family and friends, sitting before the fire with pencil and paper, while he let the needle down for seconds, sometimes just the length of one chord; each of us had to write down the name of the composer, the work, the key, the movement as well as the place within the movement. I usually scored well.

Sometimes we sat around, each with a copy of a Shakespeare play, and read the roles out loud. We played charades, too. In this I did not excel: I was too unsure of myself and not as quick-witted as the other players.

Talk at the Saunderses' seemed never to be about mundane or everyday matters or ever to fall below a high cultural level, nor did I ever hear a raised voice, a sharp or unkind word from any of them. They were, to my mind, the perfect family, the answer to my most fervent yearnings; in contrast my own family was a mess.

True, we were well-off, and I was proud of our large Tudor-style house, set back and on a corner of the residential section of Utica's main street. But we frequently quarreled, and with raised voices, sometimes even yelling at one another. I quarreled with my brother, Ernest, four years younger than I. I thought him favored and overindulged, and I hated him. Some years before, I remember having murderous physical fights during which I clawed and scratched at his face, probably wishing to annihilate him. "Why not give him some old razor blades to play with?" I once suggested, and my father was more amused than horrified—the idea was so preposterous. But I meant it.

Then there was my sister, Jo, a year and a half older—extremely pretty and so popular with boys that she became a legend among our family's friends. I was jealous of her. She was sharp-tongued and clever, and I, with my vagueness, dreaminess, and general lack of focus, was an easy target for her ridicule. I felt she despised me, and was so convinced of my own lack of worth and looks that I invariably filled my conversation with news of my sister, sure in that way to arouse interest and perhaps even win myself a friend.

Both my sister and brother, as well as my parents, seemed to be comfortable with the fact that we were Jewish, but I realized soon after I started going to school that it was definitely not an advantage. "I'm not walking with you—you're Jewish—you killed our Christ," called out one little girl on the way to school one day, and the other children followed her on ahead, sing-songing the accusation. Across the street from us, in a large white house perched on a hill, lived a girl with whom I played regularly. One day, when I arrived with my toys and dolls, she greeted me with the words, "I'm not allowed to play with you anymore—my mother says you're Jewish." At home, when I told about such incidents, my mother and father always insisted that I should be proud of my heritage, proud to be Jewish. I was not though. I wanted too badly to be accepted and liked, and if being Jewish stood in the way, I did not want to be Jewish. All my longings went in the opposite direction, and I began to think that in non-Jewish families there was no strife, no ugliness, no yelling, always good behavior and manners, everyone treating others with gentleness and care. I longed to go to a private school and, later, to be a member of the Junior League, and thus, I dreamed, a part of that other world.

Yet both my mother and father were good to me, and tried their best to be good parents as well as good to each other. And this was despite the fact that they were caught in a painfully unequal union, causing them to fight and struggle to make the impossible work—my father, the provider, struggling to make enough money to win the respect of the world at large and to satisfy the expensive tastes of his beautiful wife, in comparison with whom he must have felt inferior. And she was sometimes too clever for him. Once, when he had lost some large sum playing cards, she showed up the following afternoon wearing a new luxurious squirrel coat and matching cap. Her words then: "If you can afford to lose that much playing cards, you can afford to buy me this coat!" And naturally she kept the coat.

My father probably had a good deal of money before the crash. I remember the bold black headlines announcing it, and my father's horrified face, but my own life went on pretty much the same. When I wasn't with Frisk and his family, I was playing music with my pianist friend, Gladys, rehearsing weekly with the Utica Symphony Orchestra, and riding rented horses as often as my mother would allow. Horses—the look and smell of them—have been an interest and passion with me as long as I can remember.

I have a particularly poignant memory of my father seated in an overstuffed chair in the living room, poring over, or more accurately, struggling with, a copy of Shakespeare's *Hamlet,* wanting to please my mother and be prepared for an upcoming performance of the play. It was the only time I can remember my father reading anything other than a magazine. I believe my mother loved him, and certainly my father had lovable qualities—especially warmth and generosity—but, more important for my mother's ambition for all of us, he was good at buying and selling the jewelry he dealt with all his life. He knew nothing else, having come to America at the age of sixteen, penniless and uneducated, one of the thousands who arrived at the turn of the century. Less than ten years later he found himself in love with, and married to, a woman far above him in class, intellect, and sophistication. I loved my mother, loved her vivacity and gaiety, her good looks, and was proud of her—proud of the fact that she came from Vienna, and that her family included musicians and painters. No matter that they were not the best, they were Viennese and artists—and I have clung to that romantic image all my life. My mother represented, more than any other member of my family, a little of that other life I yearned for. It was my mother who presented me—I was scarcely seven years old—with a little violin. The gift was followed by years of forced practicing until I realized the benefits of an admiring audience as I began to show prowess and an exceptionally good tone. That in turn paid off when my father, on the advice of my violin teacher, bought me a really good violin. In due time, there followed more presents: ice skates, a tennis racket, swimming lessons with my sister every Thursday (Ladies' Day) at the Knights of Columbus pool. I was also allowed to ride horseback once a week.

As a child I remember walking far out of my way to school in order to follow a team of horses, to watch and smell them. Home from school, I remember walking blocks behind a special team of horses on their way to a vacant lot where they were plowing out the cellar for a new house. There were no bulldozers then, and each afternoon, as the cellar became broader and deeper, I watched their powerful muscles flexing and straining behind the plow. Their driver, a burly, good-natured Italian, seemed to understand me, and he liked his horses too. Once I watched with delight as, after he had watered them, he threw the remaining cooling water on their legs and hoofs. The night before my weekly ride was invariably a sleepless one, with me waiting in excitement for each hour to go by, until the wonderful moment when it was time to go to the stables, where I could watch my horse being saddled and bridled. Then, as I was lifted up, I was able to feel the leather saddle beneath me, to put my hands on the horse's neck and proudly take up the smooth leather reins—I was about to ride. But I was rarely satisfied that I had only an hour for a ride, and that the path always went around and back the same way. My dream was to find myself as the one who had to gallop for miles to get a doctor for some dying person, or to race somewhere with important news to someone who had no means of getting it except through me. And of course I was the owner of the horse in all these fantasies.

I became a good rider, with a confidence and recklessness far beyond the other, more timid riders at the stables, and I was also an accomplished violinist. "Know how to do everything well, and you will never be lonely," my mother once said. I *was* good at many things, like sports, dancing, and music, though I remember doing them mostly alone. All these activities, nevertheless, brought frustration to my violin teacher, who was planning a concert career for me. He wanted music to be my sole occupation, and was furious when I turned up for my weekly lesson with my right wrist stiff from driving a tennis ball. If my wrist was stiff from playing tennis, I must have had a tennis partner, but my memory is of a lonely childhood spent mainly with my little Boston terrier, Mickey, practicing my violin, and reading the books my mother gave me. I remember no friends.

A lonely child has fantasies, and I was no exception. What is not so usual, I believe, is to have those unarticulated yearnings and fantasies become, in adulthood, something of a reality. I was not, until very recently, aware of any parallels between my early dreams and the moves and actualities of my later life. As a child I had an ongoing fantasy that I lived in a faraway land, and though the image of that land was nebulous, my self was always clear and bright. I was unlike anyone else around me: I was a gypsy, dressed as I thought all gypsies dressed, in a full-blown skirt and flimsy colorful blouse. My hair, long, thick, and dark, fell free and was decked with flowers. I danced around on bare feet, strewing love, gaiety, flowers, and fun to all those around me. The reality, naturally, was not at all like that, but I did, all through my life, find myself dressed up at home, to be admired, in all the bright clothes and costumes and heavy jewelry I could get together, and I was often barefoot. And, come adulthood, I would live in a number of faraway lands.

With the yearning of my childhood always to be "other" and as far as possible from my own family and upbringing, it is no wonder that, to my father's bafflement, I expressed an absolute lack of interest in Harry, an over-weight young man I saw occasionally during the period I was visiting the Saunders family. Harry, I knew, was in love with me and wanted to marry me. There was nothing wrong with him, except that, for me, to be the wife of a businessman, no matter how successful, and in Utica, was preposter-ous—it meant crushing even the vaguest possibility of living out my dreams. So, even if I did spend time with Harry, I never allowed myself to get involved with him, telling myself he was not interested in the "finer things of life," like the Saunderses.

One evening, coming out of a concert hall in Utica with Dr. and Mrs. Saunders, I saw Harry out of the corner of my eye. He was standing with some friends by the side of the building, watching the concertgoers as they exited, and almost certainly with an eye peeled for me. There was no hesita-tion in my decision to pretend I didn't see him. I had to avoid at all costs the embarrassment of a greeting and the inevitable introduction. Harry belonged to my other life, and I was totally indifferent to the knowledge that he knew and forgave my snobbishness. Probably he valued qualities in me which I was scarcely aware of myself. I met with Harry at my convenience, spurned him regularly, and never allowed myself to take his affection seriously.

I did fall in love with Frisk, attracted by a stylish English accent and a vague thought that he came closer, certainly his family did, to that other life of my dreams. At any rate, I was in love, and in a way probably impossible to experience at a later age, when society's pressures and demands take hold, when thoughts of marriage, education, money, and children necessarily dilute love's essence, whatever larger fulfillment there usually is in later loves. Only after many years, almost a lifetime later, was I to know a similar love, pure not in innocence, but in final and sure awareness of the value of love without the extras that seem to be necessary in the middle years.

Nevertheless I was frightened of sex with Frisk—my mother gave me no information other than a large and often repeated NO. So there was a gradual buildup—a powerful attraction restrained by an almost equally powerful fear of consequences. We spent much time reading poetry aloud—lengthy poems by John Masefield, certainly less boring for Frisk than for me since he did the reading. And in the woods near the campus, we explored, fished for trout with our hands, picnicked, and played music on a portable phonograph. On one such picnic we lay on our backs, listening to a Brahms symphony. Our bodies formed a forty-five-degree angle, with only our heads touching. Perhaps we kissed. Some two weeks later, when my period was late, I panicked, convinced I was pregnant (did my parents not also lie together on a bed?). I was desperate with my lonely secret, and was having thoughts of suicide when I finally told Frisk. Frisk quite naturally assumed I must be pregnant by another boy. He was eventually convinced of my ignorance, and it was from Frisk, after a drive up to a hill overlooking the city, that I learned the facts of sex, delicately explained with insects and birds as examples. I was almost seventeen.

By the time I was eighteen, Frisk and I had been making love for about a year, and had reached as much of a peak in sex and love as we were ever to do. It was around then that I received my first major blow. Frisk, apparently unable to withstand the pressures and suggestions, probably from his mother and Aunt Mathilda, that he see other girls and spend less or no further time with me, told me bluntly one evening that he would not be seeing me anymore. He gave no explanation; possibly he avoided the real explanation: that I was Jewish. I do not remember the pain I must have experienced, but the details of that evening are still alive in my memory: Frisk unaccountably dressed up, white duck pants and dark jacket, making him look not only very attractive but older than his nineteen years—his more usual childish appearance sometimes embarrassed me. The evening was to be dinner at Trout Brook Inn, where I had never been: it was a rambling place, reached by way of a small bridge, on the outskirts of Utica. It was built around a lovely curving brook with plenty of trout which the inn supposedly prepared and served direct from the water. And after dinner one could walk around the grounds or sit on one of the benches near the brook—which was where we were when Frisk delivered the news which I received first with disbelief, and then shock, followed by a shameful display of imploring tears. He was strangely immovable. That event was to color and change my behavior toward men for years to come. I became wary and cagey, and made sure that I was securely loved before I ever again allowed myself the luxury of honest expressions of feelings.

Frisk came back after a few months—I never knew why—and we started seeing each other again. During the time of his absence, Dr. and Mrs. Saunders, possibly through guilt, or perhaps admiration or respect for my stoicism in not calling, frequently invited me on trips of interest: to the New England states to look at churches, to Boston to hear the Bach B-Minor Mass, and once we went to Quebec—I don't remember why. My visits continued, and always, on returning home from Skidmore for the Christmas, Easter, or summer vacations, the Hill was my first thought.

The Saunders family was a haven for me even before the series of calamities that struck my family. My sister's car accident was the first of these. It left her with a deep scar across her cheek, from ear to mouth, and may have hastened her secret marriage, secret because Donald was not only still in college, he was a Roman Catholic—both circumstances unacceptable to my parents. So the young couple eloped—ran off to Pennsylvania to marry—and came together in secret until they were formally married a year later with my parents' approval. Donald converted to Judaism, which, as I recall, meant learning enough Hebrew for the ceremony, but there may have been more to it. I don't remember being very interested or involved in the wedding, except that I did come home from Skidmore for the ceremony and my first glass of champagne.

Just before Christmas during my freshman year at Skidmore, I was also badly injured in an automobile accident which sent my father speeding from Utica to my hospital bed in Saratoga Springs, where without removing his overcoat he held four fingers before my face, asking me breathlessly to tell him how many fingers I saw. I could see them, but I had come very close to being permanently blinded. My mother never knew of the accident; she was already having bouts with the illness which was to destroy her—not, however, before she satisfied her craving to see something of the world. And go she did, on a freighter, and my father somehow managed the trip. Letters from my mother during my second year at Skidmore told of the great cities of Europe and the East, letters from Spain and France, from Jerusalem, from Egypt—and sometimes they revealed her loneliness and fear, and the spells of pain that forced her to seek the help of doctors. They were brave, beautiful, even humorous letters, none of which I appreciated until I reread them many years later.

My mother returned from Europe and lived on, in and out of bed, determined to stay alive, never letting us know her awareness of the cancer that was eating her. I see her now, getting out of bed soon after an injection against her pain. Rejecting help, she dresses herself alone and walks carefully down the stairs to the front hall, where my father is waiting. She is wearing a long chiffon dress, some dark color I no longer remember, and in spite of her thinness and the gauntness of her face, she is beautiful and her hair still thick and black. At the temple, where the dance is in full swing, people are stunned to see her—they had been expecting news of her death daily, and I watch as she dances the one dance she is strong enough to manage. My father took her home right afterward.

I didn't return for my junior year at Skidmore, mainly because of money troubles and my mother's illness. I remember feeling somewhat relieved. I didn't like studying. My first year I had majored in English literature and music, and even took a semester of Greek, probably to please and impress Mrs. Saunders, but I was not a good student. It was, certainly at the start of my first year, a revelation to find myself on my own. No one at school knew my sister, Jo, for one thing, or how plain and unworthy I was beside her. They knew nothing about me. I became, during the early part of that first year, attached to a group of girls each of whom seemed infinitely more worldy and better looking than I; but I was accepted. I became one of them and found myself less and less concerned with the miserable conditions at home and moped less over the on-and-off nature of the relationship between Frisk and me. My new friends and I were a kind of gang, moved around the campus together, did a certain amount of confiding in one another, and had a good deal of fun. I was even considered a wit. My self-confidence grew enormously, but it was not to last. One night we found ourselves sitting around together in one of the girl's rooms, and there arose the question of which church each of us belonged to. The deadly question was being asked of each girl, and I sat in quiet dread, waiting my turn and listening to each response: Protestant,

Catholic, Episcopalian, Methodist—and when I was finally asked, "What church do you go to, Alma?" I heard myself answer, "I don't go to church, it's called a temple—I'm Jewish." A burst of laughter was the immediate response—I was joking again. When the laughter died down, someone asked, "But seriously now, what's your church?" and I repeated, "I don't go to church, I'm Jewish." Their laughter was now uproarious. I was being funnier than usual. But miserable as I felt then, I kept insisting until they finally realized I was not joking, that I really was Jewish. Their disbelief turned to wariness, and I could almost feel myself somehow diminish before their eyes. They continued to be my friends; I had no others, nor did I want others, but there was a difference I was not imagining. I came to realize, after that evening, that any error or wrongdoing on my part was judged, not on its own, but as that of someone who was Jewish. I had to be more careful than the others.

My second year, I switched from English and music to physical education. I was attracted to the idea of less study, and getting credits for what I liked doing—riding, tennis, folk-dancing, swimming, team sports. Together with the ongoing string quartet I had formed soon after I came to Skidmore, it seemed ideal. It was also the major of most of the girls I was spending time with. I was unprepared, however, for the course in advanced anatomy which accompanied that major, a course which forced me to "pith" or mash in the living brains of frogs, to learn anatomy through the dissection of crates full of chloroformed cats.

Notwithstanding that I was a mediocre student at best, I do remember that second year as mostly pleasant, with each trip home to my family representing an almost unbearable contrast—my mother sick most of the time, money troubles, quarreling, and escape flights to the Hill, another contrast and the inevitable role playing.

My mother was in a sanatorium at Clifton Springs, near Rochester, the summer that my father got the call from a state trooper. I had been staying in a rooming house to be near my mother most of the summer. Frisk sometimes came to stay with me, Dr. Saunders came a few times, and my father occasionally spent weekends, when he could get away from what remnants of his business remained—almost all of his income went toward paying for the sanatorium. I happened to be in Utica when that call to my father came. "Do you have a son named Ernest?" "Yes, I do." "Well, we're calling from Oneida Lake. Your son is dead; he drowned."

My memory of those days shows me a picture of a small knot of people standing in the street around my father; I see myself in the guest room of the Saunderses', awake most of the night despite the pills Mrs. Saunders has given me; I see my father so abruptly changed, haggard, gray, and drooping—and then, driving the three hundred miles to Rochester in my mother's black Buick roadster with its elegant narrow red stripe, and telling my mother about Ernest. And I see my mother in her room after she has been told, taking a quick look at the photograph of Ernest in the locket she always wore around her neck, as two nurses help her dress. During the long drive back to Utica she hardly speaks, except for an occasional, "I've got to keep my chin up," and as I glance sideways I see her jutting her chin out and up as she says the words.

My mother lived on almost two years after that, at home, almost always in bed. Mrs. Saunders learned to know my mother then—they shared a common bond since Mrs. Saunders some years back had also lost a son of fifteen years, and there was also a growing affection.

Money became more and more scarce—such huge amounts were needed to pay doctors and drugstores, to keep my mother as much out of pain as possible. When my father could no longer afford a private nurse, Dr. Katzman taught me how to give the injections against the pain. I don't believe there was any hesitation on my part. But by then my mother's arms and thighs had been pierced so many times it was a problem to find so much as a point of unpunctured flesh. She always waited until the pain became unbearable, and then she would have to search with me, both of us peering and pressing the hard, lumpy flesh in search of a clear, unpunctured place for the needle.

I timed my own activities according to her need for injections. Sometimes I left her alone, letting myself be persuaded by her own suggestion to leave her, knowing always that she would be grieving alone for Ernest until the pain returned. I can still hear the sound of her voice calling my name. When she called at night, it was my cue to run downstairs to the kitchen and boil water to sterilize the syringe. Once I dropped and broke the hypodermic needle and had no replacement. It was around two in the morning, winter, and I banged on the doors of St. Elizabeth's Hospital, on Genesee Street, until I was finally allowed entry and then denied a syringe. Yes, they knew who I was, and they knew about my mother, but without a doctor's prescription they could do nothing. My hatred for rigid rules may have started that night. Anyway, I eventually woke Dr. Katzman and was given the precious syringe. The rest of that night is blanked out in my memory.

Another time, also late at night, I was in the kitchen preparing the hypodermic, hearing my mother's calls and groans and simultaneously the whining of my little Scotch terrier, Barley, that Mrs. Saunders had given me. Barley had chronic ear trouble. He was in almost constant need of treatment and often whined and scratched his ears. That night I remember myself suddenly spinning around in a rage and kicking him. Whatever it was—frustration, sleeplessness—I don't know, but I am apt to think of that episode when I hear or read of some forms of brutality, even the killing of a baby or small child. I remember my own capacity to act contrary to my usual self.

Through all my family's troubles, the Saunderses continued to be a solace, though now it was mainly string quartets with Dr. Saunders: Silvia and Olivia were mostly in New York or Boston, and Frisk off to Albany Law School. He hadn't made Harvard, which must have been a bitter disappointment for his family. Occasionally Silvia and Via came home for the weekend, sometimes with friends, and it was during one of those times that I was introduced to Jim Agee.

I had been hearing about him from Frisk and from Dr. and Mrs. Saunders, who referred to him as a genius. I knew he was in his last year at Harvard, that at twenty-one he already had been published, that he was a friend of Via's and coming to Clinton soon. All that I knew, but when I did finally meet him, I was totally unprepared for his extraordinary good looks. I was ill at ease with him, and painfully aware of my ignorance. I dreaded to find myself alone in a room with him, and felt wholly inadequate to his friendly overtures. In company his behavior was outrageous—he used words like *fuck* and *cocksucker,* right in the Saunderses' music room. He seemed to have no respect for the good manners and decorum everyone else adhered to—talking openly and easily about subjects no one else ever touched on: poor people, Russians, revolution. Influenced as I was by the Saunderses, I felt that literature and music were above such matters. Only years later did I realize that Jim's behavior then was partly calculated, a perhaps callow wish to shock the family and their friends out of what he saw as their smug gentility. He got away with it, though, and in fact he was respected and listened to. I slowly came to realize that Jim Agee, far from being impressed and influenced by the Family, as I believed everyone was and should be, was himself gradually becoming an influence on them. Mrs. Saunders, for example, suddenly one day embraced the idea of communism.

I was even slower to realize that Jim and Via had become a couple, and the news of their approaching marriage surprised and confused me. The thought of Jim marrying anyone seemed unimaginable, except possibly some sublime creature matching his own glamorous presence. I may even have had a vague wish, which I would not have allowed to surface, since I was still in love with Frisk, that I might be that creature.

Although present at the large reception for Jim and Via just after the wedding ceremony, I remember only the music room flooded with friends—nothing of Jim, nothing of Frisk. Via's face, however, stands out clearly: she is blushing and looking prettier than normally. I was later told that I was unusually quiet throughout the evening.

Soon after, Jim got a job at *Fortune* magazine, and he and Via went to live in New York. Occasionally they came to Clinton for a visit, and those times were generally lively. There was some serious talk, of course, but there was also fun. Jim introduced a guessing game called Metaphors in which the character to be guessed is described according to what that person would be if he or she were an object—a musical instrument, a body of water, a room, a period of history, and so on. The game provided endless scope for flights of fancy, but I know I was particularly fascinated with Jim's imagination as he described an absent friend in terms of a bathroom cabinet, Thoreau as a musical instrument, or Mrs. Saunders in terms of a landscape. Another game, or rather performance, of Jim's was his imitation of Bach's D-Minor Toccata and Fugue as rendered by Leopold Stokowsky, for whom Jim had great contempt. Jim, using only his mouth and vocal cords for sound, accomplished the bass-tuba parts with great low-pitched Bronx cheers, and the high violin passages with a light nasal "hey nonny, nonny, nonny, nonny . . ." It was uproariously funny and surprisingly accurate. Once Jim produced those sounds at my home, with my mother sick upstairs. I don't recall what occasion brought the Family, including Jim, to my parents' house—possibly I was needed at home, and they decided to go with me. At any rate, I remember how torn I was—proud and delighted with their presence, but also acutely aware of my mother, who must have heard the sounds and laughter, and was probably in pain.

A month or so after that evening, my mother went into a coma and my father hired a full-time nurse—Bobbie, who had been my mother's nurse before. Late one night, it must have been around midnight, Bobbie and I were both awake and talking together, when we heard a crash in the street outside. We ran out of the house into the street. How still it was—no traffic, not a sound, only off on the opposite corner a smashed car on its side, with one fender slowly settling, but soundlessly. I don't know who called the ambulance which came for the rest of the passengers; I only remember a young boy struggling up from the road telling us he thought he was all right, and Bobbie and me half-carrying him across the street and into our house. We undressed the boy, who was soaked with gasoline, washed him off, and left him to sleep downstairs on a couch in the sun-room. The following morning, when I went into the sun-room with a breakfast tray, I found the entire room splattered with vomit, and the boy unconscious on the floor. An ambulance came for him, I cleaned up the mess, and the hospital informed us later that his condition was critical and included a crushed kidney. This episode elicited from my father a heavy, tired disgust with me—only I could bring a dying stranger into the house while my own mother was dying. She died the following night.

When the bank took over our house, we moved, my father and I, to Sunset Avenue. It was a nice, though much smaller, house in a "good" neighborhood, selected, I am sure, because my father still had a marriageable daughter. It was a lonely life for both of us, and I was neither solace nor company for my father. I spent most of my time with the Saunderses, and though my father never expressed a dislike for them, I knew he resented them and was uncomfortable in their presence. I also played music for which my father had neither interest nor understanding. It occurs to me now that I never heard my father sing.

But my father probably did take pride and, I hope, pleasure in the feature story I wrote on Dr. Saunders which *House and Garden* magazine published at that time. I think it was both Silvia and Mrs. Saunders who put me up to it—convinced me that I could do it. There was plenty of material after all—Dr. Saunders was well enough known for his name to be in *Who's Who*, which meant a good deal in those years, and the publisher of *House and Garden,* a friend of Dr. Saunders', welcomed the idea. Silvia supplied the photographs, Dr. Saunders was on hand to advise me and give me information, and the article, as I remember, turned out to be a kind of something-for-everyone—the homey and intimate combined with more serious horticultural data. I have no idea how I managed it, but behind and throughout the effort there was very likely the determination to do well—to excel and receive praise—a characterization I have recognized all my life, one that is likely behind everything I have done. I remember being paid seventy-five dollars for the piece.

I wasn't seeing much of Frisk then, mainly because he was away at school. By then, too, we had cooled off toward each other, and I think it was around that time that he switched to his middle name, Blake, in preference to Percy or the nickname Frisk.

Except for the continuing string quartets with Dr. Saunders, I was now spending most of my time with my pianist friend, Gladys, and Harry, who was still in love with me. It seems now inevitable that Gladys and I found ourselves making plans for living in New York City, each of us happy and hopeful over the solution to our separate problems. Gladys at twenty was on her way to becoming a concert pianist, and there was not much future for her in Utica. I was lonely living with my father—felt myself at a kind of dead end—and even though I had no definite direction, the thought of the drastic change and promise that New York City offered was an appealing one.

Some days before we left, Gladys and I made what turned out to be our last effort to interest Harry in music. We begged him, "Just listen through it, give it a chance." It was Beethoven's Fifth. He sat, and seemed to be listening, his large, curly head bent toward the phonograph, and at the finish, Gladys and I looked at him, hopefully and expectantly. We gave up for good when his wry answer came: "It took just four hundred and thirty revolutions." That evening, after driving Gladys home, we sat together, Harry and I, in his car, discussing my future in New York; Harry earnestly and practically, and I with my usual vagueness or perhaps some interest. In the midst of the discussion Harry made a surprising remark: "What happens to my love? Where does it go?" Not long after I left for New York, Harry became the business manager of the Utica Symphony Orchestra. The exposure to music inevitably paid off, and Harry today, a diabetic and almost totally blind, has music, and I know it is more than solace—he is a sensitive and discerning listener.

I was scarcely settled in New York when the Saunderses proposed that I go along with Silvia to Europe. Silvia was a talented photographer, and Dr. Saunders had numerous connections with English horticulturists. The idea was to take pictures of English gardens, for publication with accompanying articles and captions in *House and Garden* magazine. I was to go because of my successful feature story on Dr. Saunders for that magazine. I don't know whether it was that accomplishment or Silvia's wish to have me as a companion that qualified me—perhaps both. At any rate, we went, and the Saunderses paid most of the expenses.

It was some six months after my mother's death that we sailed for England on the *Rotterdam*, Silvia's blue Ford touring car in the hold. I remember thinking how pleased and excited my mother would have been—a trip to Europe! I also remember having a long crying spell while at sea, triggered by memories of my mother's suffering and my own loss, but spreading out to become a deep upwelling of grief over the private agonies of animals and people, until I felt myself wallowing in it, and not without some enjoyment. I had a similar fit of crying while still at Skidmore, after reading one of my mother's letters from Europe, and then too I remember letting it purposely get away from me, even abandoning myself to the questionable luxury of being forced under a cold shower by anxious friends.

In England, thanks to Dr. Saunders' fame as a horticulturist and the letters of introduction he had sent, we had a ready welcome at each of the country houses we visited. I don't know whether or not I was successful in hiding my ignorance, but I took notes and bluffed a good deal, expressing wide-eyed interest in everything horticultural. Silvia, ten years older, more knowledgeable and more sophisticated than I, had little trouble. We spent our nights at modest bed-and-breakfast places, and during the day drove along the lovely springtime countryside, to our "English gardens," where Silvia photographed, her camera perched on a tall tripod, and I talked with English gardening people, who may or may not have thought I knew what I was doing. After we did our work, we were usually shown around the seventeenth- and eighteenth-century houses that went along with the gardens, and then invited to tea. It was after one such afternoon that we noted with amusement, as we were driving off, that we two alone among some dozen guests were without titles. Most of the gardening people we had to do with were, as I now realize, extremely patient with us, though I believe they assumed that I was at least as knowledgeable as they in the Latin names of plants and flowers. I kept careful notes, however, and we even learned a little Latin, enough to try a description of our menstrual periods as we drove along one afternoon: *Cursalorum monthalatum, floweta rosea*. We thought it quite funny.

Once, we said our formal good-byes and were scarcely out of the driveway when we burst into peals of uncontrollable laughter. It was release from tension mainly, but we were also realizing more than usual the comedy of our position, and the contrast between what we had just left—the formality, the perfection of manners, style, and cultivation of England's upper class—and what we were heading for: our usual little bed-and-breakfast room with the inevitable lumpy mattress and the landlady's cockney talk. Other countries have rich and poor, with differences in education and living style, but it seemed to us that the English alone make class distinctions discernible solely through speech. I remember Silvia's quoting someone as describing the "high" English spoken by women as the bull-and-canary accent.

Our gardens took us as far as Cornwall, where we walked through an avenue of flowering rhododendrons as high as average trees, in the garden of a man named P. D. Williams. I also remember scones and Cornish cream and a little fishing village named Mousehole, which we learned to pronounce "Mouzel."

Back in London I stayed alone for a month in a rooming house behind the British Museum while Silvia traveled to the Continent and to Germany. She explained that Germany might not be safe for me—unpleasant things were happening to Jewish people ever since Hitler had come to power. The year was 1934. I did not think much about it, but occasionally, during my almost daily visits to a nearby restaurant, I overheard some ominous talk. Once, a young woman, newly arrived from Germany, tried to interest me in what was happening. I hardly reacted—and I recall no sense of either personal threat or even identification with what she reported.

Most of that month I was lonely, even desolate, though I do have a comic memory of riding around London on a rented bicycle, scarcely knowing where I was or was going, and finding myself pedaling through high, wide-open gates, vaguely aware of a large black limousine simultaneously driving out through the portals. I was stopped almost immediately by a pair of distressed, then amused, bobbies, who sent me sailing out. I had just passed the royal family leaving Buckingham Palace.

When Silvia returned, we crossed the Channel to France—there were a few French town gardens on our list too. Of those, I recall only one, distinguished by its complete lack of flowers or even grass—all gravel, paths of flagstone, stone benches and numerous large mirrors set at intervals. *House and Garden* didn't take that one.

I was alone in Paris, too, for two weeks, but never lonely, and even walking about on my own I had a sense of belonging, which I certainly had not had in London. The French, men and women, looked at me, and that was enough. In London, no one showed the slightest interest, with the exception, of course, of the refugee woman.

Jim and Via met us on our arrival in New York, an unexpected and pleasant surprise. They were living then on Leroy Street, in the Village, only a few blocks from Bedford Street, where Gladys and I had taken an apartment. It was a warm and safe feeling to have them as neighbors, even if I didn't expect to see much of them. I remembered the discussion, before I came to New York, when everyone suggested that Gladys and I not be too isolated, that we try to find a place near Jim and Via.

Settled again in New York, I tried, but halfheartedly, to give my life some structure. Unlike Gladys, however, who gave piano lessons and practiced regularly, I was living in New York without a clear objective. I played string quartets at least once a week, and also enjoyed playing violin and piano sonatas with Gladys. I knew I was talented, but unlike Gladys I had neither the industry nor the ambition to become a professional. Sometimes Gladys played piano quartets and quintets with us. And I remember a walk-up apartment on Park Avenue, Gladys and I climbing narrow flights of stairs to play with a young violinist named Avery Fisher.

Of course I had the articles to write for *House and Garden,* and sometimes, following instructions from Silvia, I helped her develop and print the photographs she had taken while we were in Europe. Our work found a ready place in *House and Garden,* and we were paid well. Richardson Wright was the editor then, and he seemed to like everything we brought and was certainly unaware of my ignorance of either gardens or horticulture. The articles were comparatively easy to put together. Using as a framework the notes and material I had accumulated, I borrowed freely from other garden articles. I remember making lists of usable adjectives. In the same way, I had written, a few years earlier in Utica, reviews and criticisms of musical events for the Utica *Daily Press.* Dr. Saunders had taught me how to go to the public library and look up reviews of performances of standard works, in order to use whatever was fitting for my own purposes. True, I had more knowledge and interest in music than in horticulture, but in none of my articles was there much original thinking.

At any rate, the pieces for *House and Garden* supplied some income, and whenever I ran out of money I could rely on my father. Only years later did I know the hardship this sometimes caused him. It never occurred to me to look for a job, nor do I think my father, or my mother, when she was alive, expected me to. It was assumed that, good-looking, well built, talented, and accomplished in music and sports, I would eventually marry, with the burden of my keep shifting from father to husband.

Except for my partners in music, I knew almost no one, and only very occasionally had a date or accompanied a friend to the fund-raising parties for Loyalist Spain—without, however, feeling particularly involved or affected by those events. Frisk sometimes came to New York to see me, but by then, and despite my lack of experience, he seemed suddenly too young for me. I recall Harry's once taking me to someone's New Year's Eve party, after which we both, quite drunk, went to a hotel—it was the nearest I came to having sex with him. I saw a good deal of Emma during that time. Emma, Jim's sister, also lived in the Village. With Emma a friendship developed, the character of which was almost directly opposite that of my friendship with Gladys. Emma and I liked to listen to jazz, to get dressed up, and to dance. Frequently, on a Sunday afternoon, bright with spring and sunshine, we would find ourselves stepping down into a small, dark smoke-filled basement den called Nick's, where a four-man band played jazz (no dancing) all afternoon, all evening, and most of the night. Sharkey Bonano on the trumpet and George Brunies on trombone attracted us most. Sharkey was as much fun to watch as to listen to. We waited always for the occasional moment when he, improvising, would raise his trumpet on a high note and, not quite simultaneously, but somehow appropriately, also raise his right foot and then let it down, not off beat, and not on, not in syncopation either, but again somehow very aptly. Whenever that happened, all who were not absorbed in themselves or each other would howl out Sharkey's name in appreciation. It was always a thrilling moment—it meant Sharkey himself felt right, felt himself "grooving." And whenever Brunies was doing a trombone solo, he would swing his instrument in a wide arc, following close behind the backside of any girl on her way to the toilets in the rear.

Sometimes, usually on a Saturday evening, Emma and I went to a small basement Mexican restaurant, also in the Village, where they played Latin music. There we ate and then waited for someone to ask us to dance. On these occasions we often spent more time preening ourselves beforehand than we spent at the event itself. The hour and a half of preparation and anticipation was often the high point of the evening. But the dancing was fun— rumbas and tangos with real Mexicans—and if one of them wanted to carry the evening further, it was all right to decline. There was never any danger. I invariably went home alone, either from Nick's or from the Mexican restaurant, nor did it ever occur to me not to. I was still wary of sex, and not at all adventurous in that area. Yet I flirted extravagantly, and made myself as attractive as possible. When it got very late, and we were to go home together, we walked to Emma's basement apartment, where it was dark enough to sleep until two or three the following day. Emma had a job, but I don't believe her life then had much more direction than my own. I know she suffered for being Jim's sister—always in Jim's shadow. For my own part, I was probably lonely some of the time, though I don't remember being bored or particularly concerned over what might lie ahead.

2 *Jim*

I was standing on a corner of a Village street one afternoon, waiting for a bus, when I saw Jim Agee, tall, gawky, slightly disheveled as usual, and he was smiling and coming toward me. I felt my usual embarrassment on being alone with him, even for a couple of minutes on a street corner. I was tongue-tied, as always, and then I heard him ask if I would like to go up to his apartment and listen to some music. Via was visiting her family in Clinton, and he was alone—alone and needing company. Or was he suggesting I come because he was alone? If it was company he needed, I knew I was far from adequate, and to be alone at all with Jim, for any reason, was a preposterous idea. I declined, and from that time I became still more alert and wary in his presence.

After that, and for almost a year, Jim courted me. I was interested but also apprehensive. It was bad enough to get oneself involved with a married man, but this was Jim, married to Via, a friend, and Silvia's sister. Jim was married to a daughter of Dr. and Mrs. Saunders, to whom I was indebted for years of pleasure, chamber music, and travel. At the very least, I owed them loyalty. And Jim was their prize, just as Via, I knew, was Dr. Saunders' favorite daughter. But Jim's persistence and presence were very powerful. I was flattered—more flattered, in fact, than emotionally moved, certainly at first. It was flattering to find, almost every day for months and months, a note from Jim in my mailbox on Bedford Street—sometimes a love note, sometimes just a quotation: "Damn braces, Bless relaxes," or simply "Good night, sweetheart." The long telephone talks were exciting, as were the occasional evenings when the Agees invited me to supper or a party and I would go, with my troubling but delicious secret: Jim loved me, Jim who was prized, revered—Jim who was Harvard's gifted poet, Jim who was so handsome, tall, lovable and loved by everyone.

During one of those parties, someone suggested we all play Murder, a kind of hide-and-seek game. Jim unexpectedly grabbed my hand and whispered, "This way." I followed him, his hand still clasping mine, up flights of stairs, and then up an iron ladder to the roof, where we were alone. It was a warm summer night, and we had to remain there, quietly, until we were "found." We sat on a ledge, facing each other, and I can still hear that one word he repeated softly, over and over, with a slightly questioning inflection: "Dear—dear—dear." His eyes in the dim light appeared troubled. I was confused and embarrassed, but also aware that this man was attracted to me, maybe in love with me. Finally I was relieved to hear voices and someone coming up the iron ladder to find us. Then we returned to the apartment. I don't remember saying anything.

There was also the night it got too late to go home and it was suggested I stay and sleep on the couch. I did, and I was fast asleep when I felt you, Jim. You had left Via sleeping only a room and a few feet away. How dear is the memory of your kneeling beside my couch, your long torso slightly tilted forward, and your silent, gentle touch as I was slowly awakened, sensing the miracle of our coming alive to each other—all in silence, slow, tender, and so gentle, your face barely visible in the semidarkness. You stayed there, kneeling and gently stroking me, and I watched you and felt you, both of us in wonder, in silence and love, until the light of early dawn was in the room and you returned to your bed.

It wasn't long after that night that we began making love, though the occasions were infrequent. I had all along an almost frantic need for secrecy, which Jim tried to respect but did not share. I don't remember that Jim was moderate in anything he either did or felt, so to expect him to hide his feelings or actions was almost an affront. Eventually I joined in his recklessness and cared less and less who knew. Nevertheless, it was a recklessness which was particularly hard on me, despite my natural tendency toward the unconventional, and a devil-may-care attitude: I'll get through it somehow, we'll marry and that will absolve me, Olivia and Jim aren't well together anyway. The

Saunderses? That question frightened me, and I preferred not to face it. My family? Gladys? Their lives are so conventional, they just don't understand. And what about the future? Maybe Jim won't divorce, maybe he won't marry—what then? But that was a situation I simply did not face, or want to face. Despite the knowledge of upheaval all about me, with disapproval on all sides, I shut it all out and forged ahead, without thought of any future except one in which I would be married to Jim. And forge ahead I did.

I remember myself in a suite at the Waldorf Astoria, where I have gone to see my cousin Joe Mailman, from whom I want to borrow two hundred dollars. He is wealthy and I am counting on our mutual liking. Before he gives me the money, he gestures toward an open window and says, "Alma, anyone jumping out of that window knows he would drop to the pavement. Only you think you can go out the window and go up." Years later, shortly before my son Joel was born, I thought of sending Joe a note reminding him of his warning and telling him that he was right except that I did go up for a while before falling.

The borrowed money was probably for the trip Jim and I made to New Orleans. Via was away, I do not remember where, or perhaps I never knew. At any rate, Jim wanted us to spend a week together. The plan was to drive down to New Orleans, where neither of us had been, and visit on the way the sharecropper families Jim and the photographer Walker Evans had stayed with the year before in preparing a story for *Fortune* magazine. It must have been late winter, or very early spring, for as we got farther south, we stopped the car to take the top down, and later Jim took off his shirt. When I leaned over and stroked his naked chest, he smiled and, looking ahead at the road, said very softly, as if speaking to himself, "Christ, what pleasure."

We stopped at farmhouses along the way to buy eggs for the prairie oysters we practically lived on: a concoction of raw eggs, whiskey, and worcestershire sauce. Jim loved the big cities, which one drove through in those days before superhighways allowed one to circumvent them. At Birmingham, Alabama, we stood a long time one early morning above a trestle, gazing down at a maze of twisting and curving railroad tracks and railroad cars, factories and smoking chimneys. I did not understand Jim's fascination with the sight, nor did I understand the love he felt for billboards or the plain, and to me dull, wooden houses in the towns we passed through.

We spent almost half a day driving the red-clay back roads of Alabama before we came on the gray, dilapidated shack of Jim's friends, the Tingles (their name became Rickets in Jim's book *Let Us Now Praise Famous Men*). I knew they were his friends when I saw their faces light up on seeing him. Jim had told me in detail about each member of the family, and how they lived, but I was still unprepared. I had never been close to dire poverty, and the Tingles were very poor. One of the daughters, who was wearing a flour sack, trusted me enough to show me her treasures, and I waited on a straight wooden chair while she disappeared and then returned with a small match-box. I watched her pick out, with reverence, a piece of broken ten-cent-store necklace, a bit of colored glass, and a piece of a tin toy. The same young girl prepared some supper for us, which Jim and I both ate somewhat guiltily. I don't remember what it was, some sort of cooked grain, heavy biscuits soaked in bacon grease. I didn't like any of it but ate out of politeness, knowing they could ill afford to feed anyone. The smallest boy had sores all over his legs, and these were covered with flies. Jim told me later that Mrs. Tingle worked in the fields during the day and her husband was sleeping with one of the daughters. After supper we sat and stood together on the veranda, while Mr. Tingle led us all in hymn singing. I liked these people and wanted to be liked by them, but unlike Jim, I felt uncomfortable. The distance between the Tingles and me became especially striking when I made a remark about the stars that night. They flooded the sky, and I felt I could touch them, they seemed so near, just above the house. I said something, perhaps how beautiful they were, and the remark drew a blank—no one had any idea what I meant. The night sky filled with stars was as ordinary to them as their veranda, or as one another's faces.

Of New Orleans, I recall only the graceful grilled ironwork of the houses, a disappointing search for New Orleans jazz (we did not know our way around), and being broke. I tried without success to cable for enough money for the return trip (probably to my cousin Joe), but Jim's wire for help, I do not remember to whom, was answered with funds, and we could start back. The drive to New York was faster than the trip south but of no less interest or fun. We did a lot of night and early-morning driving, sometimes sleeping in fields along the way, and once we swam in a river. One very early morning, I think it was in Ohio, is particularly sharp in my memory. On a dirt road, we were approaching a main highway empty of cars, just the sun, newly risen, shining across the white swath of the highway, and as we approached we watched with delight a lone turtle in the middle, crossing slowly, its head stretched out and as high as it could go. Then, with appalling suddenness, a large car sped out of nowhere and disappeared, leaving the turtle, in seconds, smashed and dead. Jim stopped the car and held me while I cried hysterically for a while. Perhaps he cried too, I don't remember, but I do remember the hour or so of silence between us after we started on our way again.

As we approached New York City, I began to think of my future. I was still in love, but stronger than that was my concern to survive. What now? I began to reveal more than usual my depression and worry over what was to happen. At my door on Bedford Street we on our return found Barbara Kastner, Joe Kastner's wife, both good friends of Jim's. She waited as Jim and I carried my luggage upstairs. He then went off with her to meet her husband and Via at a bar in the Village. From the downstairs landing just before she left, she spit out one ferocious word at me: "Bitch!"

That one word typified the reaction of everyone around me to what was happening to Jim, to me, and to Via. Jim and I did finally live together—beginning when Harper & Brothers gave him a small advance to expand into a book the piece on sharecroppers that *Fortune* magazine wasn't printing. He wanted a place, away from New York, where he could work in peace. And he wanted me to come out and stay with him. It was not an easy decision, for I knew that living together would, in those days, fly in the face of everything society and family not only counseled but demanded. Only marriage would eventually vindicate me, at least in the eyes of society; meanwhile I knew I was risking the breaking of ties with family and friends.

Gladys was aghast and furious, and though she remained my friend, she was unable to hide her intense worry and disapproval. I avoided any contact with the Saunders family, accepting that when they finally knew, it would be the end of my relationship with them. My sister, Jo, married and living in Binghamton, was relatively uninterested in what her "crazy" sister did. Only my father, aware of the disastrous step I was determined to take, did not drop me, though his shame must have been extreme. I remember his asking me to keep my secret from his new wife and friends in the small Pennsylvania town where he was living. I went on, nevertheless, knowing I was going into a void, with Jim my only friend. Why did I do it? Partly, the final step can be explained by one thing's leading to another, since I was in love, but I believe a larger factor was my natural tendency to move ahead, to take on what was dangerous but pleasing, with a lurking sense that somehow it would all turn out all right and that if it did not, well, I could somehow pull through even so. I had a great deal of confidence in my inner strength to get through anything. It was also typical that I scarcely looked farther ahead than a few months. But when I finally did make the leap, and moved to the house on Second Street in Frenchtown, New Jersey, to be with Jim, it was without conflict, without consideration of anything except being alone with him, and free.

The house, which had two floors, an attic, and an enormous kitchen, was rented unfurnished for one year; after that, we expected to return to New York, with Jim's work on the book completed. We went to a local auction to bid for furniture that would be pretty and not too expensive. I remember only a graceful wicker rocker and a huge four-poster, but we must have bought more than that. When we bought the bed, we had not realized that its size made it impossible to get into an upstairs bedroom. So it stayed in the kitchen, the biggest room in the house. What a delicious novelty, and how strangely cozy to lie at night in that enormous bed and look over at the large coal stove, barely visible in the dim light. It reminded me of a similar happy sensation I had had as a small child in sitting out in the street in my mother's easy chair, where it had been placed to make room for housecleaning: a delightful strangeness—the familiar in an unexpected and incongruous setting. But sleeping in the kitchen turned out to be more than just fun. During the winter months it made sense, since the kitchen stove gave off more heat than the iron stove in the living room.

When Jim started to write in earnest, it was at night and for hours at a time. I knew how fiercely he disliked any interference with his work. That and an awareness of my own inadequacy kept me away from him then, except when he wanted to read his work to me. A break from the long stretches of work frequently meant testing passages upon me, and I would listen, invariably deeply moved, sometimes not fully comprehending the long, complex sentences, but hearing them as if they were music. I believe Jim liked my lack of literary sophistication. I did respond, probably accurately, to the meaning of the words, though I had no criticism to offer. I was never particularly interested in the literary discussions that took place during visits from Jim's friends: Robert Fitzgerald, the poet; Walker Evans, the photographer; and Dwight MacDonald, the editor of *Partisan Review*. To my best knowledge and memory, Jim scarcely revised or worked over anything during those months of almost steady nightwriting, and more than once he commented, with a mixture of pride and amusement, on the enormous callus on his right middle finger, a rough, yellowed lump almost the size of a marble.

Daytime was a little like playing house. We did the housework and cooking together, neither with any regularity. When I cooked, it was always with immense ambition and no knowledge (it never occurred to me to consult a cookbook), and Jim's response to an occasional taste test was invariably, "How about a little lemon juice?"—always offered with an air of unprecedented discovery. There was one dismal dinner I prepared on the occasion of Walker Evans' first visit. I managed to ruin everything except the boiled potatoes, and that is all I remember of the meal itself; but clear and warm is the memory of Jim's smiling acceptance of my failure, and his obvious anxiety that I not be hurt by Walker's stoic silence, a silence that seemed to be shouting, "See? She can't even cook!"

I was both shy and afraid of Walker. Since he was Jim's best friend and intellectual peer, I wanted almost desperately for him to like me, and yet I intuitively felt a fatal gap between us. Walker, with his hyperrefined intellectual and artistic tastes, would never understand who I was, any more than he could, or perhaps even wanted to, understand a side of Jim that was distasteful to him at the same time that it amused him. Walker loved Jim, and could easily, therefore, tolerate and smile at what he saw as Jim's bohemian antics: the excessiveness of his loves and hates, his sometimes violent manifestations of contempt for middle-class mores and niceties, and his general sloppiness. These were all characteristics that endeared him to me, though I was occasionally alarmed by them too. What Walker esteemed and valued above all else in Jim was the artist, and he could accept and approve of me only if my understanding and estimation were on a similar plane. Of course I knew Jim was an artist—even, I felt, an important one—but I simply did not value that above all else, nor was it what I cared for most in Jim. I believe now that Walker was genuinely baffled by the lack of intellectual exchange between Jim and me as well as by the ease that existed between us.

When the weather was warm, we swam in a creek on the outskirts of Frenchtown, or played tennis. During the winter months we played cards and board games, checkers mostly. Sometimes we drew each other, slowly, painstakingly, always surprised by the discovery of new, hitherto unsuspected details in the other's face. Jim's eyes would no longer be laughing, or tender, or just looking, but suddenly opaquely blue, intense, even cold, and I was challenged to reproduce that look with a piece of lead pencil. I would try, at first seeing the look as stemming from the intensity of his concentration on my own face. But behind the intensity and concentration I found I was witnessing a rocklike hardness and coldness that made me feel lonely—it was a part of Jim I could never know, and was, perhaps, unknowable even to him. So I left the eyes and tried for the sides of his face, which I knew so well, the cheeks which always seemed so surprisingly slack when I touched them.

We also listened to records and played music together, I on the violin and Jim on the piano, inexpertly but enthusiastically botching through, among other works, the first movement of Beethoven's violin concerto. In every place where Jim and I lived there was a battered upright piano. Jim's playing resembled his way of playing tennis. Hampered by lack of training, every once in a while he transcended his technical limitations with spurts of sheer physical and emotional bravura, with brilliant results. His forehand drive, when it did hit home, was a challenge to the best of tennis players, and his flights of dramatic eloquence at the piano more than made up for his many near and outright misses.

It was scarcely a week after I had moved in that a small group of well-meaning church ladies came to our house. Jim was working when the bell rang, but I purposely waited for him to answer the door. I knew he had forgotten to remove the ribbon I had tied in his hair some hours before—a dainty blue bow, dead center on top of his head. I watched him as he stood facing the women one step before him. He was leaning forward, his long torso slightly stooped, as if deferentially—the way he usually stood when talking to someone with whom he felt shy or uncomfortable. And all the while, as he earnestly expressed his anxious regrets over whatever we were being invited to, the blue ribbon was bobbing about on his head. After the women left, I suggested he look at himself in the mirror. He groaned an unbelieving, "Oh, no!" and though he wasn't angry, my amusement certainly surpassed his.

Jim had a grown beard at that time, by no means the commonplace it is today. Even Jim's usual two-day stubble was conspicuous, though I liked it, preferring it by far to those occasional clean, close shaves which always made his face look so unexpectedly small and vulnerable. The decision to let the beard grow was a joint one, and it turned out to be an absorbing project, almost as though the beard belonged to both of us. As it grew to more than just stubble, and could be named *beard,* we were surprised to find unsuspected colors not at all matching the dark brown of Jim's head hair—reddish, black, brown, and even gray. I called it plaid. It grew and grew, to a heavy, full-blown, never-trimmed beard. I am as sure now as I was unconcerned then that it caused a good deal of talk among the neighbors. I remember someone's asking me—sincerely, I believe—whether my husband was a member of the House of David, a team of Jewish baseball players who all wore beards. I also recall someone at our front door one day who asked me if my father was home.

Eventually Jim had enough of the beard, and the clearing of his face became a project that lasted for some time. It was Jim's idea to shave it in degrees, turning each trimming, and his face, into a replica, as nearly as possible, of some historical or fictional character. There were the inevitable muttonchops of Dickens' Mr. Pickwick, there was Abraham Lincoln (Jim was a natural for Lincoln, with his tall, awkward frame, rugged features, and deep-set eyes), and finally there was Robin Hood, the funniest, with a ridiculously sharp little goatee.

The final, complete shave was crowned with the kind of haircut I usually gave him, with Jim sitting on a straight-backed kitchen chair outdoors, just back of the house, a white bed sheet draped around him and clasped behind with a large safety pin. I see him there now, and feel renewed love for him—the Jim who could relax so easily into the very simplest of human acts, all gentleness, free of self-consciousness, and without a trace of pretense. The other, more complicated Jim, the Harvard intellectual, I was never quite comfortable with. And Jim, aware of the split, occasionally expressed his own preference for what he called the farmer in him, a quality which was instinctively recognized by the tenant families in Alabama.

After a few weeks we became aware of mice in the house. They lived between the walls and occasionally came out of a couple of holes they had made in the floor molding. We didn't mind them. We knew they got food from the paper bag of garbage in the kitchen. They didn't bother us, but occasionally they bothered guests, especially Helen Levitt, a photographer and friend of Walker's. I used to stuff the holes upstairs with wads of paper when I knew Helen might be staying the weekend.

There were six mice in all. I knew because I watched them often, and I believed I could tell them apart. I was more interested in them than Jim was, but he was amused and believed me when I told him one evening how the mice had trusted me enough to chase one another around the living room. Perhaps they did not know I was there.

With our neighbors we had little contact. That was mainly the result of shyness as well as an instinctive awareness—which our neighbors may have shared—that we were different. We obviously did not do as they did, and did what they would not dream of doing. Despite the lack of communication, however, the news did reach Jim one day that a man living two or three doors away had a very special plant that produced but one blossom each year, and that only at night. It was a night-blooming cereus, and would be in full bloom that very night. I see us now quietly shuffling along in the warm dark, part of a long, slow line of neighbors. There is hardly a whisper as we slowly walk past the long side of the house and down a narrow path in the backyard, in the direction of a light. A marvelous fragrance begins to fill the air as we get nearer to the light, which turns out to be a lantern held by the owner of the plant. He is seated on a kitchen chair, one leg crossed over the other, the lantern resting on his knee and tilted so as to cast its light on the flower. The heavy, sweet fragrance becomes stronger as we approach and see its source— a large, very beautiful bloom, star-shaped and startlingly white in the lantern's glow. The man's face is lit up, along with the flower, so one can see the superior expression of ownership: my flower—I grew it. I saw that same expression again years later, in a photograph I still have of a Mexican peasant on whose land a volcano suddenly broke through the earth. His face, the face of a poor and hard-working peasant, is also bright with the pride of ownership and, almost, it seems, the pride of creation: my land—my volcano.

As the year moved deeper into summer, we frequently went for late evening walks or rides, usually as a break from Jim's work or when he was feeling good about something he had written. Once, during one of our late walks on a deeply quiet and peaceful night, we veered off the road onto a moonlit field where we lay down and looked up at the stars, hardly speaking. We made love there, and lay awhile again side by side before we got dressed and walked quietly back home, listening to the sounds and smells of night— the hum and whirring of insects and tree crickets and the sweet smell of hay and faded flowers.

Another night, when Jim had been working upstairs for hours and I was still awake, he came down to read aloud what he had been working on. It was a piece about his childhood in Knoxville—nothing to do with the Alabama tenant farmer. He was pleased with what he had written, and I was, as usual, moved by it, and wholly uncritical. Then he suggested that we go out for a ride, late though it was. We drove with the top of the Ford touring car down, the mild breeze in our faces. As soon as we were on a deserted road, I stepped out on the running board, holding on to the car door. The warm breeze turned to wind as Jim drove faster. Wanting suddenly to be free of my clothes, I pulled them off, using one hand while the other clung to the car door. As I threw the last of whatever I was wearing on the seat beside Jim, I saw his smile and realized that he understood how I felt and what I wanted. His foot stepped down even farther on the gas pedal so we might go as fast as we reasonably could, and I can almost feel again the soft warm wind caressing my whole body, and my hair, in those days long and black, blowing out behind me and occasionally tickling my back. Today, when I see the little remnant of a running board on my VW beetle, I am apt to think with nostalgia of rides on real running boards, but in particular of that midnight ride along a deserted road in New Jersey.

The afternoon we saw the baby goat we were out for a walk. Newly weaned and motherless, he was bleating in the middle of the sidewalk as we approached. We were both charmed by him. I picked him up in my arms; Jim found the owner, bought him, and we walked happily home, the goat still in my arms. There was a little stall in the backyard, and the little goat turned out to be useful as well as charming, for he nibbled the grass in the yard until it resembled the well-kept lawns of our neighbors. He was a joy to watch, with his handsome black-and-white markings and innocent, tender young goat's face. At dusk he would always put on a splendid act, kicking up his hind legs, running like mad around the yard, prancing and bucking, while Jim and I stood just outside the kitchen door, watching him and laughing together, for his show seemed just for us. But the goat bleated oftener as he grew older, wanting more and more attention. The insistent crying began to disturb Jim when he was trying to write. Eventually we let the animal into the kitchen, which always quieted him, if only temporarily.

It was the goat's insatiable longing for company that prompted us to take him along to New York one weekend. Walker Evans had invited us, but he was not expecting a goat. We had it all figured out, however: the goat could stay on a little piece of roof outside the window of Walker's apartment on East 92nd Street, and we didn't think Walker would mind. The morning before we left, I tore up a great deal of grass and placed it, along with the goat, on the backseat of the car. I didn't see that as a particularly strange thing to do, especially since it was unthinkable to leave the goat alone for so long. But I was not prepared for Walker's horror and disgust when he saw us climbing the stairs, hauling goat and grass. I now suspect that Jim, who knew Walker's fastidiousness, anticipated his reaction.

I remember the single rectangular room of Walker's apartment. The floor was covered with straw matting, and the walls, painted an unrelenting hard white, were bare except for one small photograph by Walker near the far end of one of the long walls. For furniture there were a cot, a couple of chairs, and the desk, an expensive and elegant object made of some kind of blond wood. That was all it would have been, an expensive, elegant desk, had it not been for the numerous cigarette burns along one edge. Walker had no ashtrays; the burns, from his own cigarettes, were the result of deliberate carelessness. This he admitted in wry, bemused words encompassing both his admiration for the desk as such and his contempt for whatever it represented—probably upper-middle-class good taste. I was bewildered by both the cigarette burns and Walker's explanation, and also by Jim's apparent understanding and approval.

Back in Frenchtown, we began to realize that our goat's loneliness, which expressed itself in constant bleating, was becoming a serious problem. We decided that a companion would be the solution, and Jim suggested going to a farmers' auction, which would be interesting and fun in any case. A few days later we found a country auction not far from Frenchtown, but all they seemed to be selling were cows. One cow after another was brought up onto a platform, where the auctioneer, a heavy, muscular man, yelled out its merits. I disliked him on sight, and was especially upset by his method of getting the cows to turn around to be viewed from all sides: he simply twisted their tails until they whirled about. He was so matter-of-fact, with never a glance at the cow, that she might as well have been a piece of furniture on casters. No goats were in evidence, and we were beginning to worry. Suddenly one was led onto the platform, but it was nothing like the lovely creature waiting for us at home. Here was a gaunt dirty gray animal, obviously no longer young. But it was a goat. Jim bid, and the goat was ours. We drove home, the goat in the backseat of the car, and it was not until we had them together that we realized the extent of our thoughtless naïveté: what was needed was a female goat. The two of them got along all right, but the crying merely doubled in intensity. The situation became intolerable; after days trying unsuccessfully to find a home for our goats, we put them in the car and drove, silent and ashamed, to the local butcher, who was naturally pleased with the gift.

In thinking now of that one year we spent on Second Street in Frenchtown, I realize that my most vivid memories are happy ones. And yet it could not always have been like that. When I look at the volumes of chamber music, which I still have, all bound in Frenchtown by hand—the complete string quartets of Haydn, Beethoven, Schubert, Brahms, Mozart—I can hardly imagine I was ever capable of such meticulousness, patience, and neatness; I can only infer that I must have been driven by loneliness or boredom. What did bewilder me was my own lack of ambition despite varied talents, as compared with the vast energy and drive that streamed out of Jim. There was never any question of where Jim was going or what he was to do with his life. The answer seemed to have been there always.

of dilapidated shoes, and a piece of wood whittled into a makeshift spoon. I tied the bag together again, leaving it as nearly as possible in the position it had been dropped, and waited for Jim to come home. When he returned, the tramp was following him. Jim looked pleased as he came in the door and explained that the shelter was there all right, but was already closed for the summer. And so the hobo, whose name was Walter Clark, was to stay with us and remain our guest for the next two weeks, when we would drive back to New York.

Walter Clark was an extremely quiet man, with a natural humility that was free of subservience. His eyes, a pale clear blue, gazed with serene gentleness at the surrounding world, intelligently aware but without much interest, and not a trace of sadness. I do not recall his speaking at all, but he must have talked some, or at least answered some questions, because we did learn a few things about him. He had been on the road for twenty years or more, all over the country, hopping trains, occasionally doing odd jobs or some panhandling, but rarely staying long in one place. He ate and slept mostly beside bonfires, along with other hoboes, in the woods or near the railroad tracks. During the last years, though, he had been tramping it alone, and not entirely out of choice. The younger men tended to stay clear of anyone who was getting old and therefore threatened to be a potential responsibility. When Walter Clark could no longer hop trains with ease and began to realize his buddies were beginning to avoid him, he traveled less and less frequently, and during the previous couple of years the area around Frenchtown had become his home. He liked whiskey, and on Saturday nights he could always count on one or two free drinks in a local bar. During the winter months most towns had shelters where the homeless could find some warmth, hot soup, and sometimes a hard-boiled egg. He had lived for a while in an abandoned chicken coop, until some small boys found him and stoned him out.

One afternoon we took him to the movies and then to a restaurant. The movie was a double feature, with a Mickey Mouse cartoon after the first show. Surreptitiously, Jim and I watched Walter Clark's face as he stared at the big Hollywood treatment of beautiful upper-class men and women moving about and emoting in elegant surroundings. Whatever impressions he had must have been beyond even confusion, for his face throughout remained utterly deadpan. But the Mickey Mouse cartoon brought him to life—and there was a faint, not-quite smile on his face all the way through. Once, when Mickey suddenly looked down, his little body suspended between two mammoth cliffs, his mouse face expressing horror at his predicament, we heard Walter Clark's quick intake of breath in fear and identification; he emitted a virtual sigh of relief when Mickey Mouse reached the other cliff in safety.

The restaurant was on the main street and had booths. We sat in one of them, Jim and I on one side, Walter Clark facing us. He was obviously baffled by the magnitude of choice on the menu Jim handed him, because he almost immediately put it down, and sat incuriously, without looking around, with his steady, serene, peaceful expression. If he had ever been in a restaurant, it must have been many years before, yet he did not seem embarrassed or shy.

Jim picked up the menu and began to read it aloud, inviting Walter Clark to select the meal that sounded best to him. After listening to most of the long list, Walter Clark finally made his choice—the one item that had lit up his eyes: pork and beans.

I wanted to adopt him. We had rented a summer place not far from Flemington, where we intended to leave our belongings while we were in New York. I thought we could simply drive him there and leave him, with cans and cans of pork and beans—he would have a place to stay and we would call him the caretaker. But Jim, unlike me, saw the future responsibility this would inevitably bring, and which he did not want to face. So it was agreed that Walter Clark would have to leave when we did.

With a few days left, it dawned on us both that we were also leaving the mice, which had by then become trusting and nearly tame and would surely be trapped or poisoned by the next tenants. We had planned to hire a small truck to move our furniture to the little stone summer house. I was determined not to abandon the mice, so we agreed to take them with us. I bought an enormous "ketch-em-alive" trap in town, and we worked earnestly on the rescue operation until almost four in the morning of the day the moving truck was to come.

We didn't sleep, because we had to wait for the mice to come out for food. They were used to the lure of a paper bag and would nibble a small entrance through the paper. When the first mouse appeared and chewed its way inside the bag, we immediately placed our "ketch-em-alive" trap outside the bag's hole. Unfortunately, we hadn't realized that a year's worth of coddling had fattened each mouse to a size slightly larger than the entrance to our trap. So, as each one appeard—and it seemed forever between mice—we had to reach into the bag and push the mouse through and into the trap, from which it was emptied into a tray that was quickly covered with a window screen. We finally got all six, but one ran off and there was nothing more to be done.

We left Walter Clark in the house the next day while we drove over to the summer place with the truck. I wanted to ride in the truck, so I climbed up with my tray of mice and sat next to the driver. The driver asked no questions, and I offered no explanations, especially after his first astonished glance at the mice and then at me. When we arrived at our destination, I told the driver of my intentions; I can clearly see his dumbfounded expression as he watched me carry the tray of mice into the house and let them run off in all directions. How sorry I was a few months later when I found, in the ruined sleeve of my best woolen coat, a nest of baby mice.

We were packed and ready to leave for New York just a day before the year's lease on the old house was officially up. The electricity had already been cut off, but we had the whole day and the three of us did some last-minute cleaning. I can still see Walter Clark with the broom he held so awkwardly, and the slow, dreamy way he swept, with that infinitely gentle and remote look in his eyes. One felt like either laughing or crying over him, but either reaction would have been as out of place as annoyance or anger.

I don't remember whether we addressed him as Walter or Mr. Clark, but he had entered deeply into our lives and thoughts those last two weeks. We couldn't take him with us, but the question of how to leave him, and with what, or how much, was seriously debated. It was eventually decided to leave him pretty much as we found him, or he us, but a little richer. Jim bought him two quart bottles of whiskey and I went to the ten-cent store, where I purchased a tin plate and a set of eating utensils. Then we bought a half dozen cans of pork and beans, and some matches and candles. Very carefully Jim explained to Walter Clark that since he was our guest, he had a right to be in the house after we left, lights or no lights, until midnight the following day, when the lease expired.

That evening, as we were about to leave, we said our final good-bye. He was sitting on the floor of the kitchen. He had lit two of his candles and placed one at each end of his outstretched legs. Seated there on the floor, his legs spread far apart, he was looking, not at us, but at his presents—the bottles of whiskey, the tin knife, fork, and spoon, the plate, the cans of pork and beans. Perhaps it was the light from the candles that did it, that gave the picture of Walter Clark seated on the floor before his treasures an aura almost holy. Of course it may have been simply pleasure over his unexpected acquisitions, or he may have been drinking from one of the bottles. It was possible, too, that what we were seeing was, at least in part, the love he had come to feel for us, and we certainly had for him. One more year, he had told us, and he would be eligible to enter an old men's home. He was fifty-nine.

After Frenchtown we lived in Brooklyn for a while, on St. James Place. Jim was writing a story on Brooklyn for *Fortune* magazine, so of course living there was convenient. We were given the use of the house, completely furnished but unoccupied at the time, by Jim's good friend Wilder Hobson. I hated the place: four dark narrow floors full of stuffy furniture, and an oversized kitchen in the basement. I felt lost and alone there most of the time, and disliked the idea of having to keep it clean and tidy. I was particularly miserable with the heavy, dark furnishings. I don't believe I've ever felt more misplaced.

An average Saturday night meant a party of drink and dancing in someone's apartment. These nights brought together close friends, pretty much of an age and of a kind. Married, mostly, around twenty-nine to thirty-two, some worked on magazines of the Luce type or in publishing houses, some were free-lance writers, with maybe a teacher or a painter or a musician or two. The records played were always "hot jazz." There was, as Jim wrote in an unpublished film treatment set in that place and time, an "easy, casual and very unserious kind of promiscuity among these people; the kind which rarely if ever goes beyond kissing and fondling in the kitchenette or the room where all the coats are piled on the bed."

When the weather became warmer and the Brooklyn story was finished, we went to the summer place we had rented near Stockton. It was an old stone house, set plunk in the middle of a field. There was no running water or plumbing or electricity, but we had a well, a huge fireplace, and an outhouse which the two of us painted white. We both loved that house, and the times we spent there together were gentle and peaceful. I especially remember the large kerosene lamp on a round table, and its lovely soft, warm glow. We did everything by its friendly light: reading, working, making love, talking—it was preferable by far to the efficient glare of electric lighting.

Sometimes we had visitors. The poet Delmore Schwartz arrived one early summer afternoon for the weekend. I found him pleasant enough, but morose, and clearly interested only in talk with Jim. So except for the meals I prepared for them, their time was spent mainly in literary and philosophical discussion, in which I did not have the remotest interest. Helen Levitt came out one of those days and did try listening for a while, and even interposed a question, which Delmore somewhat rudely repulsed. I heard the exchange, felt sympathetic with Helen and, I remember, somewhat annoyed with Jim for apparently going along with Delmore's attitude. Helen took pictures of both of them that day. I, meanwhile, was anxiously concerned for a number of cows in the next field—I was convinced they had no means of obtaining water, and I remember pumping pails full of water from our well and lugging them to each of the five or six cows in the pasture. Jim, who loved hats, wore his newly acquired railroad cap the Sunday afternoon we drove Delmore to the train, and Helen took a picture of the three of us—Delmore in the backseat looking his usual sullen self.

I looked forward to visits from Joe Kastner and his wife, Barbara. Barbara, pleasant and pleasant-looking, and her husband, redheaded, jolly, and boyish, both clearly adored Jim. I think what I liked most about Joe and Barbara was their marriage—there was a sureness about their relationship, a quiet confidence in themselves and in each other, which seemed superior to other marriages I either knew or had heard of.

One day when Walker was alone with us, Jim suggested that the three of us make love together. The idea was not at all agreeable to me but, idealizing Jim as I did, I went along with it, believing, as I think Jim wanted me to believe, that the suggestion was not to be understood as a lark, but as a genuine wish to bring together the two people he loved most. He also quite possibly thought, knowing my reservations about Walker, that all would be resolved in that act of intimacy. What Walker thought or felt about me I can only surmise—possibly jealousy, quite certainly bafflement at Jim's interest in and love for me. Sexually he probably thought me attractive, though I, on the other hand, had no such thoughts of Walker. The "experiment," however, did not last long. Less than five minutes after the three of us, naked on the bed, had begun tentatively to fumble with one another, Jim realized it was a mistake, that he did not want it. It was too late, though. He slipped off the bed and removed himself to a chair in the corner of the room, where for the next few minutes he sat crying—agonized sobbing it was, and I can only guess the reasons: probably a combination of love, jealousy, despair, and self-hatred, and possibly, knowing Jim, a generalized world grief. Walker and I soon disengaged ourselves and left to dress. I remember no talk or discussion about that incident—either then or later.

The times when Wilder and Peggy Hobson came were mostly fun. Wilder, a tall and handsome young man who wore his clothes easily, got his name from his cousin Thornton Wilder, author of the play *Our Town* and the novel *The Bridge of San Luis Rey*. Jim and Wilder played into each other's wit, and the results were always hilarious, with even the most banal remarks made somehow special by one or the other. Perhaps it was drinking together which loosened their hilarity, though I don't remember excessive drinking on either side. "Roll Out the Barrel," for instance, which was popular at the time and constantly being played, became especially funny when each chorus was turned into a new triteness: "Roll out the barrel, Nothing succeeds like success," and so on. Jim and Wilder outdid each other in thinking up impossible and absurd names for people and places. Wilder shared Jim's interest in New Orleans jazz and was then writing a book on jazz, a book which has since become a respected and sought-after account of that music in the thirties. Peggy, with her wide-set brown eyes and pert nose, was doing secretarial work for Muriel Draper, a well-known salon woman. Since I had never had a job or earned money myself, I was particularly impressed by Peggy's work.

Thinking back, I believe that my only source of relaxed confidence at that time was my physical self. I was good-looking, healthy, and well built and, in company, relied almost solely on those attributes. Only alone with Jim did I feel secure, sure of his love for me and what I believed was his deeper knowledge of who I was.

When we were alone together, there were no literary discussions, but Jim often read to me, from his own writing, and from those writers and poets he most loved and admired—passages from Blake's *The Marriage of Heaven and Hell*, and from Joyce, Faulkner, Hart Crane, François Villon. His tutoring even covered classical music (in which I was trained), and jazz, which I believe we both liked equally. But mostly, I was enormously influenced by his largeness of spirit and simple, direct humanity—not that I didn't have such tendencies of my own, but they might not have developed without Jim.

My understanding of Jim and his work was instinctual rather than intellectual, and since we were both highly intuitive, there was, at our best, a rare and unspoken understanding between us.

Toward the end of the summer, Jim told me of a coming visit by his friend Father Flye, an Episcopalian priest. As the time of the visit approached, I became more and more apprehensive. I was both interested and uneasy at the thought of meeting a priest and having to address him as Father. Father Flye, I knew, lived in the South, and he and Jim had corresponded since Jim was a student at the St. Andrew's parochial school, where Father Flye taught.

Knowing Father Flye's importance to Jim, his approval seemed essential, and I wanted badly for him to like me. Before Jim drove off to meet his train, I suggested that I change clothes—the day was warm, even hot, and I was wearing what was then called a playsuit, a skimpy cotton affair, sleeveless, bare midriff, with bloomerlike shorts. Jim drove off saying, "No, don't change—you're fine just as you are—just be yourself—don't worry." Jim returned with Father Flye in the car, and I saw a much older man than Jim, tall, with a furrowed face and a reversed collar. As they approached, I noticed Father Flye discreetly remove his arm from around Jim, a gesture which confused me. Then, on meeting Father Flye, I almost immediately sensed his disapproval and even jealousy. The three of us talked awhile, light talk as I remember. Then I left them alone and went off to put together what I had prepared beforehand for a meal.

With something like shock, I realized that I neither liked nor trusted Father Flye. Why? I asked myself. Jim wanted us to like each other, and I knew that initially I had felt open toward him, as I did toward all Jim's friends, hoping to be liked. But I couldn't rid myself of the discomfort I felt with what seemed to me a fatuous, even unctuous, quality in Father Flye's "goodness." But I respected what I knew to be his sharp mind and extensive knowledge, and in consideration of the two men's mutual regard and caring it seemed better not to tell Jim of my reservations. Although Father Flye's visit was of some hours, my recollection is almost totally one of discomfort and bewilderment. Just before he was to leave, he asked me to kneel with Jim to receive his blessing. It was in our little makeshift kitchen, and as I dutifully kneeled beside Jim, the wooden floor hard beneath my knees, I felt the awkwardness of what I was doing, its falseness. Out of the corner of my eye, seeing Jim, I had a fleeting thought of the strangeness of a grown man in a kneeling posture. Father Flye knew I was Jewish—why did he insist that I kneel? Why did I acquiesce, and why did Jim so easily assume I was in agreement? True, I had a minimum of religious training or experience, but the act of kneeling to be blessed by a priest with whom I felt such discomfort, even mistrust, was possibly one of the most awkward and hypocritical acts of my life.

Kneeling was not foreign to Jim, whose childhood was interwoven with the Episcopalian high church. But all through the years of our relationship, I saw his struggles with the church—he would have rooted out its influence if he could have, and more often than not he hated its power over him. Jim was religious, but his religiousness was of a kind that seemed far removed from any institution. Years later, Walker Evans wrote, "His Christianity—if an outsider may try to speak of it—was a punctured and residual remnant, but it was still a naked, root emotion. It was an ex-Church, or non-Church matter, and it was hardly in evidence. All you saw of it was an ingrained courtesy, an uncourtly courtesy that emanated from him toward everyone, perhaps excepting the smugly rich, the pretentiously genteel, and the police."

It is a superbly accurate description of Jim's religiousness, which, like his politics, was completely personal and individual; it was impossible to imagine Jim belonging to any organization or adhering to any doctrine.

Over twenty years later, I met Father Flye again. It was with my son Joel, then just twenty years old and looking not unlike Jim at the same age. Father Flye, clearly entranced with Joel, invited him to an event the following evening at Madison Square Garden. Joel went, and told me later that it was a right-wing rally in support of France's claim to a colonial Algiers. After the rally, in conversation with Joel and with David McDowell, a publisher and a friend of Jim's wife, Mia, Father Flye had spoken of the many worthwhile ideas coming from the Right, and had said that Hitler, despite his crimes, was a man of superior intelligence and much maligned. My reaction at that time was a kind of inward satisfaction that my earlier impression had not been unfounded, that Father Flye, though a good man, was not *that* good.

It was late the summer after we had left Stockton that I realized I was pregnant—by no means a happy realization. I had known for years, since before Jim's marriage to Olivia, that he feared the ties of family—anything which might interfere with his writing. I knew that was the reason he and Via had had no children, and I was convinced that having a baby was almost certain to be the end, perhaps not of the marriage itself, but of the core or essence of it. Jim received the news with violently mixed emotions. To have a child with me was a wish fervently and frequently expressed while we were making love, but I always knew it to be an emotion of the moment. Once pregnant, I knew I wanted the baby, but not at the expense of losing Jim. I thought I had resolved the difficulty when I went secretly to a doctor and received an injection which was supposed to induce a miscarriage. Jim's reaction, on hearing of the act, was totally unexpected. No two ways about it, he wanted us to have the baby, he knew for certain, he had no doubts. Was there any way to reverse the effect of the injection? The injection failed to work, and convinced now that Jim wanted the child, I relaxed and began happily to make plans.

We found an inexpensive apartment near the Village on Fifteenth Street—only one flight up—with ample room for us and the coming infant.

I liked being pregnant. I was healthy and confident in myself and in Jim's love for me and my growing belly. Friends, mainly Jim's friends, had many recommendations for prominent and expensive obstetricians, but I remember feeling confused by the number of choices. I finally opted for a program offered by the New York Hospital, not only because it was cheap—the total cost was only sixty dollars—but because, unlike most women, I liked the idea of a different intern for each examination and a faceless or unknown doctor for the delivery. I had heard of the exceptionally high standards of the interns at New York Hospital. I lied during the interview to establish my right to a service meant primarily for the very poor.

It was a happy time, with Jim showing an almost equal interest in my growing and changing body and in sustaining his own feeling of newness in love. The apparent need to recapture and hold the freshness and newness of "love at the beginning," always to feel alive toward me, showed itself all through our relationship. He often, for example, kept himself from completing the sex act, purposely withholding from himself an orgasm, in order to prolong, sometimes for days, the feeling of passion, alive and needing. Once, long after we were married, we were on our way home from an evening with friends when Jim suggested we spend the night, instead, at the Hotel New Yorker—scarcely a subway stop from our apartment. I agreed, but at the desk, even before Jim signed the register, the man in charge denied us a room: we not only had no luggage, but by a quick glance at my ringless fingers he saw we were not even married—and about to commit a sinful and illegal act at the New Yorker hotel. We left, took the subway home, where Jim packed a suitcase full of dirty laundry while I slipped on the necessary wedding ring. The proper trimmings then displayed, we returned to the New Yorker and the same clerk, who then, deadpan, allowed us a room.

It must have been some time around the third or fourth month of my pregnancy that Jim, wanting again to recapture the feeling of newness, came home one afternoon with a large corsage, a white gardenia. He pinned it on me, and invited me on a date. We kept up the pretense of a first date during a long, bumpy ride on top of an open Fifth Avenue bus. We had climbed up to the open level and bumped along until the end of the line, paid another fare, and rode all the way back to Fifteenth Street. All New York streets were two-way then. Soon after our return, I began to bleed, and the young internist at New York Hospital insisted on two weeks' bed rest in a hospital. Since I was not supposed to have any money, he recommended Bellevue, where I had to remain for the entire two weeks, even though the bleeding stopped after a few days.

Those two weeks were a revelation. I had never before been close to misery. Harlem Hospital, I was told, was overfilled, and patients had spilled over into Bellevue, where the women's section was so overcrowded that the beds were lined up along the corridors. The beds themselves were hardly adequate: one of them, I remember, was held together with pieces of scraggly rope, and in my own bed, one of some sixty in the gynecological ward, I had my first experience with bedbugs. The nurses were unpleasant, and seemed to go out of their way to deny or delay the simplest services—even toilet paper. They were all white, while almost all the patients were black—which could easily lead one to believe their behavior was racist, but I have since witnessed the same shameful behavior at a nursing home where the relationship is reversed: mainly black nurses caring for black and white patients. The nurses at Bellevue received then, I was told, very little pay, but the black nurses at the nursing home I know of are members of a union which guarantees them relatively high earnings and benefits. Of course there were, and are, exceptions, but it is hard not to draw some unpleasant conclusions relating to the care of the sick and helpless poor. It is easy to spoil the already rich. The pedigreed dog automatically receives superior care.

In the bed next to mine was a young black woman who, like me, had had symptoms of miscarrying. Her husband, dark-skinned, sweet-faced, and serious, arrived each evening after work, and I listened to their soft voices as they happily discussed the coming baby. Then one night, it must have been around two in the morning, I heard her moaning softly and crying to herself, clearly in pain. I rang for a nurse, who arrived carrying a flashlight held down until she reached the young woman's bed, then flashed it full in her face as she asked what the trouble was. There was no answer except for the low, pained crying. When I explained the possible cause, the nurse disappeared without a word and returned with a bedpan. For the next fifteen minutes I listened to the young woman's low cries of pain and despair, while the nurse silently held the pan under her body until, the miscarriage over with, she left with her covered pan. She gave not a single word of comfort.

Back with Jim, the pleasure of being healthily pregnant continued, with little thought beyond that of the coming child, until, near the end of the eighth month, Jim, meaning well, I suppose, made an extraordinary suggestion. We were in the kitchen, Jim watching me as I was preparing some food for us: "What do you think of our having separate places . . . it would enhance the times of our being together . . . just as an experiment . . . what do you think?" Accustomed as I was to deferring to him, to accepting, almost as gospel, his every suggestion, and knowing somewhere inside me that I had given up my own life, even my family, and had staked everything on him—knowing and thinking all that, I remember keeping silent when he made his suggestion, with my insides churning in fear and heavy despair. I was about to give birth, and wanted a home, intact and with Jim. I know I didn't show the extent of my fear and despair, nor do I remember what I answered, but we remained together on Fifteenth Street until the pains began and Jim drove me to New York Hospital. There I was left, with nurses and interns in charge of me, until, sixteen hours later, the baby was born and I was taken to the maternity ward. Husbands, in those days, were normally not around until after the birth.

The day Jim called for me and the new baby, he arrived, smiling and happy, with a gift, a wide-brimmed straw hat he had bought at Woolworth's and had trimmed himself: it had prettily arranged multicolored cloth flowers around the brim. There was also a new pair of black patent-leather pumps with three-inch heels—which I wasn't supposed to wear. He forgot the baby clothes we had bought some months before.

At home, I became almost overnight a "mother," while Jim, despite a growing interest in and love for the new infant, made no changes in his usual routine of all-night work and talk with friends. We scarcely saw each other, and then, less than a month after my return from the hospital, he told me he had been sleeping with Mia Fritsch, a *Fortune* magazine researcher. Jim prefaced the announcement of his affair with the fervent wish that we be clear and honest with each other, so that nothing might come between our love for each other and the baby. I was, he assured me, the "center" of his life. I was totally unprepared for the announcement. We were sitting near each other, Joel asleep in another room and I on our one large easy chair, contentedly crocheting a brick red coverlet for the new baby. Helen Levitt's mother had taught me to crochet, and I was proud of the foot or so I had completed. Jim spoke the words quietly, and I stopped my work to listen and look at him. How clearly I remember my shock and disbelief. But there was more, for he went on to tell me—in response to my faltering questions—that he and Mia had been to our apartment and used our bed while I was in the hospital. My reaction was instant and automatic as I leaped across the space between us to strike him, in wild fury and pain.

The following months were wretched ones, mainly because of my own fear and jealousy, not at all alleviated by Jim's constant assurances that it was "only an affair" and that it would be over soon if only I would let it run its course. But Jim's words and restatements of his love for me and Joel did little to calm me.

Of course there were periods of well-being. We listened to and played music together, made love, occasionally saw friends, and took walks with the baby, to whom Jim was becoming more and more attached. I was a good mother. To me, that meant anticipating every possible want or need to ensure the baby's uninterrupted welfare. I changed him almost before it was needed, and at the first signs of a whimper I nursed him. The baby almost never cried, but even then it was a short-lived affair, because I don't believe any mother could have done better than I in thinking of every possible detail and ultimate reason for discomfort. Joel was a glowing and happy baby. I do, however, remember leaving him alone—once for over two hours. Of course he was nursed, sleeping, and clean, and I did my usual checking and anticipating of every conceivable contingency; nevertheless I did leave him alone, and thinking back, I believe it was partly a need for free time with Jim, and partly a wish to be and act as I believed Jim wanted me to be and act.

Jim had a horror of the variety of motherhood exemplified in excessive anxiety and propriety, so I tried always to downplay anything that he might construe as overanxiousness. Jim himself hated any form of mothering—he did not want to be controlled, and he was particularly on guard against the subtle kind of control that takes the form of loving solicitude, often on the part of women. Aware of the need to protect his individuality, I kept carefully away from any infringement of that right. I also kept clear of his work, and ran immediately to him to tell of anyone's even slight attempt to influence him, or his writing, through me.

Jim's feelings about controlling mothers, particularly toward their sons, may have stemmed from his experience with his own mother, a highly religious woman who tried, perhaps quite naturally and understandably, to lead the child Jim along the narrow path of her own religious morality and its uncompromising laws of right and wrong, without realizing that she was dealing with an unusually imaginative and rebellious child. Jim never forgave his mother for taking him firmly by the hand, one day, to be circumcised. He was eight years old. The reasons, he was told, were medical, but he suspected, as he told me, that the procedure was supposed to prevent excessive masturbation.

In a short, six-line satirical poem, Jim sets his feelings down in unconcealed bitterness:

Mumsy you were so genteel
That you made your son a heel.
Sunnybunch must now reclaim
From the sewerpipe of his shame
Any little coin he can
To reassure him he's a man.

In his wonderful foreword to Helen Levitt's collection of photographs *A Way of Seeing*, he comments with extraordinary accuracy of feeling on the various images. His comment on one is particularly piercing: a photograph of a moment in the life of a fat, somewhat unhappy-looking child of perhaps ten years. She is seated on a box in the street and is almost succeeding in lifting a smaller child, a boy, to her lap. The boy, his back to the camera, not quite but almost resisting, is clearly much too old for even an adult lap. Jim's words: "The children . . . are already engulfed as deeply in the future as in the present or past, and I know of no record of man-eating motherhood more accurate or more fearsome."

I remember clearly the decision to leave the baby alone once for almost two hours—a decision which hung on whether or not to accompany Jim and some friends on a round of the Village one evening. There was no question of Jim's staying behind, and I simply wanted to go along. It was at a place in the Village that we stood watching couples dancing, not having yet decided whether or not we wanted to stay. And Jim, succumbing finally to my entreaties, danced with me. It was possibly the only time he ever danced, and I was acutely aware of how awkward and lovable he was and looked, his face contorted with the effort of mastering something he had never done, with someone he knew loved dancing and was good at it.

But I was mostly at home alone with the baby. Often Jim came home at dawn, and there was no way I could tell whether it was a deadline he had to meet, making it necessary for him to remain in his *Fortune* office, or whether he was up all night talking with friends, or more likely, I imagined, with Mia. I became obsessed with jealousy, and the quarreling became more and more frequent—always interspersed with passionate lovemaking, tearful apologies and promises, more recriminations, and more and more lies, until I felt myself becoming both bitter and desperate. I was desperate because I felt I had no options: I was still nursing the baby. Of course I wasn't always alone, and I do remember the ease and pleasure of caring for and playing with Joel—a happy and healthy baby can give a lot of pleasure. I also had occasional visits, mainly from Jim's sister Emma, Helen, and my own staunch friend Gladys, who has remained an unjudging friend through all the years. But I did spend long hours alone during the day and at night, and I can still smell the corned beef and cabbage steaming up from the Irish bar just beneath our apartment, and hear everyone's favorite tune from the jukebox, which never seemed to stop: it was "Roll Out the Barrel," played over and over again. No one seemed to tire of it.

I was much too proud to show the self-pity that was consuming me, and I scarcely dared admit, even to myself, that the marriage with Jim was failing. It couldn't fail, partly because I had nowhere else to go, and the more desperate and lonely I felt, the more I behaved in a way to bring about just the defeat I feared. It was almost as though I wanted to lose, wanted defeat, because my actions and words seemed calculated to drive Jim further into a situation he kept insisting he was trying to escape. And so I fought, and cried, and felt almost triumphant with each discovery of any weakness or lie in Jim which could add fuel to my fury and outrage and fill me with even more indignation. Finally, when Joel was almost four months old, I made a decision. Of course, it was a decision which very possibly affected adversely a helpless infant, but it was a decision prompted by enough loneliness and desperation to make it, for me, the only possible one.

I was about to nurse the baby, my breasts full and ready, when Jim walked into the apartment. I still remember his half-smile of greeting, and how he threw the summer jacket he was carrying over onto a chair. His shirt was wet with sweat, which told me that he had been walking fast, and had probably run up the one flight of steps to our apartment. It was late afternoon, and I neither knew where he had been nor questioned him, but suddenly, and on an impulse, I rose from the chair where I was sitting and held the baby out toward him. "He's your child too, Jim," I said. "You find a way to feed him from now on. I'm not nursing him any longer." Jim's two arms came out automatically to receive the baby I placed in them. And we stood facing each other—Jim, tall and gawky, a hurt, quizzical look on his face, and I, more and more determined, though my breasts were aching. "How? What should I do?" he asked, and I mentioned a clinic a few blocks away which would advise him. Then I abruptly left the apartment. There was no hesitation, regret, or even feeling for Jim's predicament, or the baby's, for that matter. I was mainly concerned with finding relief for my hard, aching breasts—with only a slight thought, painful and poignant, of how easy it would be to retract my decision, easy for me, easy for Jim, and above all, easy and right for the baby. There was no pausing, however, on my way to the drugstore nearby, where I bought a breast pump. Ten minutes later, I was back in the now-empty apartment, and for the next hour or so, in the kitchen, I was pumping out as much milk as I could: I never nursed Joel again.

The rest of that year was somewhat easier, partly because I was freer once I was no longer nursing, and the three of us went out together more often. Sometimes I even left the baby with Jim, once for three days when I went, with Helen, to North Carolina to visit her brother Bill, his wife, Janice, and their first son. My memory of that weekend is mainly of worry that Jim would fail to follow the long list of instructions I had left for the baby's care. But I also remember learning to play the guitar then—almost an entire night spent practicing songs requiring the four chords I had learned. That was a one-night acquirement I displayed with pride to Jim on my return.

One night an unexpected visit from Whittaker Chambers, a friend of Jim's, interrupted Joel's last feeding for the night. As Whittaker walked up the one flight to our apartment, I saw he was staggering, and very drunk. "Jim is working," I told him. "I don't know when he'll be home." He came in, and made his way to our one comfortable chair, his large, lumpy body almost falling into it. I meanwhile went to the back of the apartment to finish with the baby and put him to bed for the night. When I returned, with a pot of coffee and two cups, I thought Whittaker was sleeping. I was mistaken, because almost immediately he began to talk, his eyes half-closed. It was garbled, drunken talk, scarcely understandable, and then he began to cry, sometimes sobbing outright, as he mumbled his fears of the Russians. "They're after me," he sobbed over and over again. I did not understand much else, mainly because I wasn't that interested. Rather, I was feeling acutely sorry for him, whatever the problem was. Whittaker Chambers was a colleague of Jim's—through *Time* and *Fortune*, where Whittaker also worked. No one seemed to like him, Jim had told me, and Jim, who found something to like in everyone, had befriended him. It was almost dawn when Jim finally came home and I, happy to be relieved, went to bed.

The baby was a continuing delight, and I loved watching Jim feed him and laugh with pleasure and pride at his every advance. But Jim continued to see Mia, and the lying went on, as did the recriminations and quarreling. Twice I tried to run away, one time taking the baby on a subway to Emma's apartment on Houston Street; the other time I simply grabbed the baby and ran from Jim, down the stairs and out of the apartment, without knowing where I was going. Jim ran down and out to the street after me and pulled me back—and I think in each of us then there was an awareness and appreciation of the particular comedy of Jim's way of dragging me back up the stairs by my long hair, caveman fashion. And through it all I knew that Jim loved me, loved the growing baby, and was even still in love with me. As for me, I knew that even though I still loved him, my main emotion was the need for security, for myself and the baby.

In my growing despair, I ate less and less, smoked constantly, and realized that not only was I losing an alarming amount of weight, but my hair, possibly the feature I was most proud of, was rapidly falling out, to the extent that bald spots began to appear. I no longer remember where or from whom the suggestion originated, but it was decided that Helen Levitt and I together, with a car my father gave me, would travel down the coast by freighter, the United Fruit Line's, to Mexico, where we would stay for three months. It was a welcome idea. Helen was interested in taking photographs in Mexico, and I very obviously needed to get away. Helen minded my determination to take the baby along with us. "Who wants to travel with a mother?" I remember her saying. But I was willing to take a chance on the baby's remaining healthy rather than leave him behind in Jim's care.

Muriel Rukeyser, a poet friend of Jim's whom I particularly liked, and who I knew liked and understood me, came one evening to tell us about her recent trip to Mexico. Muriel gave me the address in Mexico City of a friend of hers, a recently arrived refugee from Nazi Germany who was also a pediatrician. That address later catapulted me into a complete change of being and living, a change so drastic that I have since wondered whether there might not be more than blind chance behind such seemingly chance events.

It was not more than a few weeks before our boat was to sail that I found myself, baby in arms, in Jim's office on the twentieth floor of the Time-Life Building. What I was doing there I no longer remember, but I certainly remember my own harsh resistance to Jim's pleas that I change plans and stay—that three months was too long, anything could happen, that he could and would change and all would be different. I remember the stubbornness and contempt which must have shown on my face, and how Jim, striding over to the open window, threw one long leg over the protective glass, turned, and looked back at me defiantly. I answered his look with equal defiance, even contempt, before I turned and left through the open door and walked down the corridor to the elevator. It was at the elevator that I suddenly thought, "Oh my God, what have I done? I've forced him to do it—he can't now *not* jump," and I turned and ran back to the office, through the still-open door, and empty office, to the open window. I looked down, twenty floors down to the street below, expecting, I suppose, to see a sprawled body, a crowd, I scarcely knew what, but traffic way down there was proceeding as usual, and I turned back—to face Jim hiding behind the open door, a sheepish look on his face.

It was easy for me to view Jim as a scoundrel during that year, and in some ways I still do. But I know that my condemnation embraces only a partial picture. Moreover, the dynamics which go into any relationship are complicated enough to be, perhaps, never fully understood. Nevertheless, and even with Jim no longer here to defend or explain himself, I mean to try to examine that relationship.

We were both what was then called bohemian and unconventional. My own unconventionality, however, or sense of rebellion against society, was different from Jim's and didn't go as far. First, I was a woman, which meant I had to be more careful, and my unconventional tendencies had to be necessarily kept in check, so that I went, or tried to go, only just so far as was becoming or acceptable to the few around me that mattered or who were, themselves, in varying degrees, rebels. The skills and talents I possessed were for my personal pleasure, or more important, served as an allure or additional attraction and were not to be pursued as a career. I was perhaps twelve years old, but I still remember my mother's answer to my violin instructor's request that he be allowed to "take me in hand," sure that I was concert material. Her reply left no room for discussion: such a future was unthinkable—"Alma will get married one day."

Jim, as a man, highly educated, an artist, and with the driving force of his art, possessed a self-confidence which I was far from having. Not that Jim didn't have his limits, but they went far beyond my own. I don't believe Jim gave his ordinary behavior much thought, any more than he gave thought to what he wore.

In general, however, I remember feeling comfortable with Jim's ways, which were basically not unlike my own, certainly before the birth of the baby. I was naturally lax in the ways of conventional living, and fell easily into the habit, with Jim, of eating, making love, and sleeping when we felt like it. I cooked and kept house irregularly and probably badly, and dressed mainly to please Jim and myself, never to satisfy a current fashion. Nevertheless, there were, occasionally, suggestions and ideas from Jim which showed me how far apart we sometimes were on some issues—suggestions to which I silently agreed, partly not wanting to disappoint Jim and to expose a deep-seated need in myself for conventional behavior on some matters, a need I believed might run counter to Jim's way of perceiving me. A case in point was Jim's suggestion that he and I and Walker have sex together. I believe that that suggestion of Jim's was an example of his personal need to live and feel intensely, to perpetuate as much as possible that intensity, and to compromise that need as little as possible. Jim was probably unaware, certainly at the start of our time together, of how far different from him in that respect I was. In the beginning, Jim may have had a need to justify the intensity of his infatuation with me by projecting onto me qualities which I did not fully possess. And I, flattered by the projection, and wanting to satisfy and please him, allowed him his illusions. Perhaps we were not all that different, but our differences were great enough to cause trouble, especially after the birth of the baby, when I became immediately true to myself, to my own and the baby's needs. Of course, Jim's wanting us to live in separate places toward the end of my pregnancy was selfish in the extreme—he had undoubtedly already begun his affair with Mia. But Jim's and my behavior during the entire year after the birth of the baby was, in general, I believe, an acting-out of our true selves. Jim was an experimenter—a man of ideas. He was bursting with them—ideas for movies, for writing, for living, for loving, for being—and he wanted to try them all out, on himself, on any willing person near him. He was utterly indifferent to what was proper or correct, and seemingly unable to conform. Yet he was exceedingly kind, and intent on not causing the slightest pain to anyone, by either word or action. In the light of Jim's behavior during our last year, that last statement may seem implausible, but the overall picture is true. Jim suffered through the hurt he caused me, but it was not in his nature to conform to my needs and demands, any more than it was in my nature to accept and live with what I saw as an unconscionable betrayal. The English poet and mystic William Blake spoke directly to Jim with the aphorism "Sooner murder an infant in its cradle than nurse unacted desire."

But I had my own desire—and it was powerful: the overwhelming need to have Jim faithful to me, and a father to our child. And I fought with every

My mother

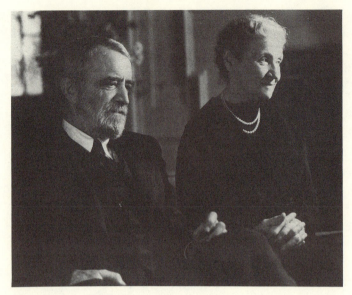

Mr. and Mrs. Saunders

My family, with me at the right

In New York, 1938

With James Agee and Delmore Schwartz in New Jersey, 1938 or so

© 1993 *Helen Levitt*

James Agee in New Jersey, 1939
© *1993 Helen Levitt*

Bodo in Mexico, shortly after I met him

With Joel in Mexico, 1943

Bodo with Joel in Cuernavaca, 1946   In Cuernavaca, 1946

Together for the passport that took
us to Germany.

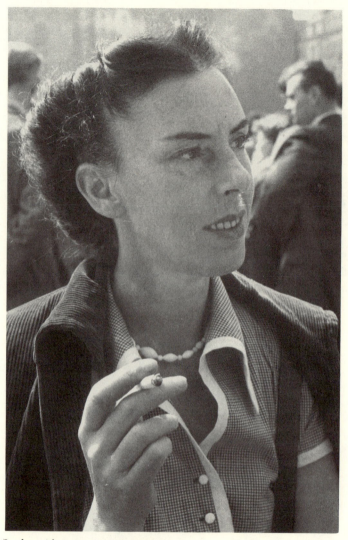

In the mid-1950s
Photograph by Eva Siao

With Bodo in Berlin, early 1950s

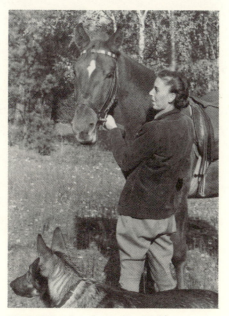

With Roland and our dog, Rolf

In Ahrenshoop, summer, 1951

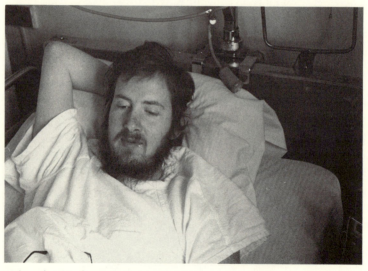

Stefan after his first attempt at suicide

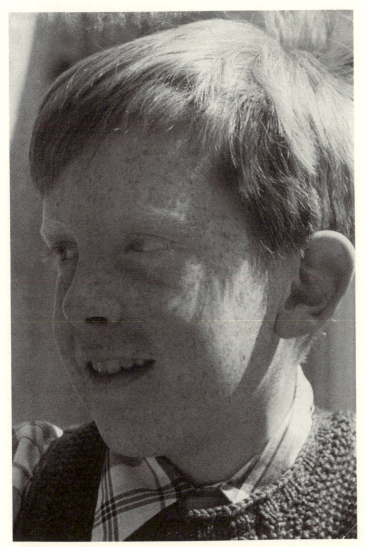

Stefan

4 With Bodo in Mexico

*F*rom almost the moment that the boat started to move, I was looking ahead, thinking of events on the boat, the baby, the approaching meal, and even Mexico, that strange country where I had never been. Jim, and my life in New York, became almost immediately of the past. And so I believe it is whenever one finds onself moving toward another place, city, or country. There is a moment when the past is gone and the future becomes a part of one's living, almost before it is there. I still had thoughts of what had been, but such thoughts slowly receded and the future became more and more alive. The sea air, the roar of the boat's engine, the bustle of the crew, the other passengers—all seemed to work together to give me a new and unexpected interest, even excitement, as if I suddenly became awake. And when Helen and I went with the baby for our first meal on board, I discovered, to my amazement, that I was hungry—and I ate well for the first time in many months.

The boat sailed gently down the coast, almost but not quite out of sight of land. Joel, confident, healthy, and beautiful, with his silky blond hair and fiercely blue eyes, gave pleasure to everyone on board. I remember sprawling on the wooden deck and playing with him while Helen, a few feet away, took pictures of us both. An unexpected docking at Cuba one evening allowed us the extra bonus of a short taxi ride through Havana and a fleeting impression of smiling black faces, music, lights on the colored stucco of the houses and a gigantic building, probably a hotel. Once the antics of a group of dolphins fascinated us for hours—they leaped about and played just in front of the advancing boat, cleverly avoiding anything on the boat's underside which might injure them. They infected us all with their gaiety.

There was also, I recall, a middle-aged Mexican gentleman who always sat and ate with us at our table, and who seemed intrigued with me and the baby. Once he placed his hand gently on my knee under the table, while I, just as gently, removed it. The same man, I remember, accompanied us during our first supper in Veracruz and helped us with the language.

My absorption in and fears for the baby probably account for my nearly complete lack of memory of Veracruz, or even the drive to Mexico City. I had been warned of the dangers of bringing a year-old infant to Mexico, but I was confident that Joel's basic good health, together with my constant care, would be sufficient to ward off any illness. My sharpest memory is of a Sterno can and its flame, over which I heated Joel's food during one of our stops on the drive to Mexico City. I must have had some impression of the spectacular mountains then, though I remember only Helen's statement "It's all so familiar—I've seen it all in the movies." And I agreed with her, she has since insisted. That is strange, because now, each time I find myself in Mexico, I experience again, and as something new, the violence and grandeur of the Mexican mountains.

As we drove nearer to Mexico City, it became clear that Joel had developed diarrhea, just the condition I had been warned of and which I was so sure I could prevent. By the time we reached the outskirts of the city, there was no thought of finding lodgings for the night. The baby needed a doctor urgently, so with the help of a dictionary, kind strangers, and the precious address Muriel Rukeyser had given me, we found our way directly to the home and office of Dr. Rudolf Neumann, who, fortunately, was at home and who, fortunately, spoke English.

Joel was to have a long siege of an intestinal infection, which could have taken his life had it not been for the persistent and unstinting care given by Dr. Neumann, who, I later discovered, was one of the two best doctors then practicing in Mexico City. My subsequent dismal experiences, and negative attitude, toward doctors have invariably excluded Dr. Neumann, who will forever remain for me a supreme example of the ideal in a physician, combining knowledge and experience with compassion, intelligence, and simple common sense.

Looking back, I know I neglected Joel during the weeks that followed, absorbed as I was then in my own changing life, and trusting too much in the baby's basic good health to pull him through. Dr. Neumann, aware of my seeming inability to realize the seriousness of the situation, took me aside one day and flayed me with words strong enough to reduce me to tears and to bring me up short with the knowledge that I was, indeed, dealing with a life-and-death situation.

But that was weeks later. The first day of our arrival at Dr. Neumann's office, I was unaware of any seriousness in the baby's illness, and my main memory is of a handsome young German we met there. He was sitting on a table, one foot beneath him and the other swinging back and forth, as he introduced himself and questioned the two strange young American women. He had the impossible name of Bodo Uhse, but I liked his looks and the way he was dressed: the casual sport jacket, the shirt collar carelessly open, and his slender body—it all seemed to go along with the delicate structure of his face, with its aristocratic nose under wide-set pale blue eyes. He told us, then, almost nothing of himself except that he was a friend of Dr. Neumann's and had been in Mexico for a year. I was less curious about him than Helen but welcomed, as she did, someone who spoke English and could show us around. And in the car my father had given us for the trip, the four of us drove around Mexico City, then as bright and beautiful a city as it is possible to imagine.

I can still close my eyes and see again, and feel again, the crispness of Mexican mornings, the clear, thin, sun-filled air, the blueness of the sky, and always the two snowcapped volcanoes, like jewels, which one could then see from almost any part of the city—Popocatépetl and Ixtacihuatl, whose Indian names always seemed to proclaim the pride and glory of Mexico and her marvelous cultural past. I remember our driving the entire length of the lovely Paseo de la Reforma, with its broad walks and lawns, and around each rotunda, with a varied and always beautiful monument within a circle of grass, the three of us marveling at the stunning layout of the city, and Bodo and I recalling Paris and the similarity with the Champs Elysées. There were often groups of donkeys on the streets of the city then, and even on the Paseo de la Reforma one would sometimes see a half dozen hungry little burros under heavy loads of firewood, their slim little legs trembling under the weight. I didn't like that side of Mexico—the cruelty, the ignorance, the poverty. I simply could never get used to it. And yet I cannot forget the loveliness and the brightness that was Mexico City in the forties.

Helen and Joel and I were then living at a hotel which, though outwardly decent enough, was plaguing us with bedbugs, and I was particularly concerned for Joel. Bodo recommended that we change—to a place where he frequently went horseback riding, an old ranch on the outskirts of the city, which had recently been modernized and took tourists. The Rancho Blanco turned out to be, for each of us, something like a realized dream. I still know the name of the owner—Manuel Elizondo—who greeted us with a smile and a flourish of his wide-brimmed sombrero. Manuel, slim, handsome, and elegant, always wore the traditional Mexican charro outfit, and it took me a while to realize that his charm, his outfit, and in fact the entire Rancho Blanco were all calculated to attract North Americans, which, of course, they eventually did—*eventually*, because, as we soon realized, we were the first to enjoy the newly renovated structure which had been a run-down and deserted colonial ranch.

The exchange then was five pesos to the dollar, so the cost of staying there was relatively low, though by Mexican standards it was exorbitant. Helen and I were each given a large room leading out onto a long, wide balcony, which looked out on the grounds below. In my own room was a crib for Joel, which seemed to include some half dozen handsome long-braided, dark Indian girls all vying for the chance to help with the blond baby. My bed, an immense waist-high colonial four-poster which Manuel told me had been occupied by Cortés himself, was equipped with three wooden steps on each side.

We had scarcely gotten settled when we realized that the excessive bustling-about of the dozens of servants was in preparation for an event which was to be very special indeed: a day set aside for the entertainment—Mexican-fashion—of a large entourage of Hollywood actors and actresses. I have no idea what was paid for that day, but one's imagination can soar, since of the attractions which we were fortunate to witness, along with Mickey Rooney and others, was the famous Los Voladores, a flying spectacle performed by Indians brought for the occasion from their native Veracruz.

More extraordinary by far, however, was the fact that the Indians had consented at all to the performance, done normally only once a year and only in their native state, just as it was conducted many centuries before by the Aztecs, on a pole at least a hundred feet in the air. I didn't see the pole when it was brought and planted deep in the earth, but I know that was how it was done, just as I learned later of the complicated process involving the winding of ropes for the flyers, and the making, at the top, of a little revolving platform and frame. The platform wasn't more than two feet in diameter, and yet the musician (who accompanied the four flyers on the climb up the rope ladder to the very top of the pole) danced there—danced on that tiny platform, playing a flute and small drum, doing little intricate steps which we could scarcely see from down below. The four flyers each perched on a corner of the frame and began to wrap ropes about their bodies for the flight. They were magnificently dressed, with brightly colored feathers around their bodies and coming out of their peaked hats—a marvelous sight against the clear bright blue of the Mexican sky. The flyers at some unseen signal simultaneously let their bodies fall backward, headfirst, each twisting the rope around one bare ankle. Was I afraid for them? I don't remember, but I know I was in awe. It was a feat simply to have climbed so high, and to so small a platform. I have heard since that a mishap or miscalculation is not at all unusual. We watched, painfully craning our necks, until we realized that we should move far enough away to see the four of them gracefully descending, in ever-widening circles, slowly floating around the pole, or rather, soaring, because they did resemble grotesque birds. They made what I later learned were thirteen revolutions in all, and as they reached the last, they each somersaulted and gently landed upright on their feet. What I remember finding particularly remarkable was that the musician at the top so correctly calculated the distance and time as to slide down one of the ropes and land on the ground at the same moment as the four flyers. I don't remember their faces, but I clearly remember the strong, impassive face of the Indian who remained on the ground the entire afternoon, continuously striking a drum, with the same rhythm, over and over and over again, so that the sound of those seven notes, or tones, and their subtly complicated rhythm has been inside me ever since.

Bodo was a frequent visitor at the Rancho Blanco, and Helen and I both knew it wasn't just for the horseback riding. Bodo was a writer, we learned, and Helen had concluded he must be a Communist, and that that was why he did not introduce us to his friends. When the three of us wanted to go off together, the baby, still not well but not seeming unhappy, was transported in his crib to the enormous kitchen in the back of the ranch, where he was usually surrounded by some half dozen women of all ages, all anxious to care for him. I had by then learned enough Spanish to relay Dr. Neumann's strict instructions. It was a good arrangement, I thought—until one day I was offered a cup of coffee in that kitchen. The coffee was brewing in a large clay olla, or urn, on top of the *bracero,* a small charcoal-burning stove in one corner of the kitchen. One of the women dipped her ladle into the dark depths of the olla, brought it out, and poured it into my cup through a small sieve. On the sieve I saw not only coffee grounds, but the unmistakable bodies of little black flies, some still squirming. After that experience, which coincided with Dr. Neumann's talk with me, I remained in constant and strict attendance on Joel.

I was perhaps five feet away from Joel one afternoon, vaguely aware of the dappled shadows of the bougainvilleas on the crib where he sat playing. I watched as he casually reached out to pick up something small and dark lying near him on the white sheet. I don't believe I have ever moved faster, for my leap forward to snatch the sheet off and away from the crib was simultaneous with the sudden awareness that Joel was about to pick up a deadly scorpion. My movement—quick, automatic, and complete—left no time for even fear, and only afterward was I aware of the awful consequences my act had prevented.

It must have been about that time that I became aware that Bodo was attracted to me, and almost at once, with that awareness, I started to think of not returning to New York and Jim. It was a welcome and hopeful thought, because Bodo began to appear as an excuse—a reason for not returning to an intolerable and seemingly unsolvable situation with Jim. I had never expected to meet a man who could match in any degree Jim's largeness of spirit or his prestige as an artist, or even his good looks—but here was Bodo, a European who spoke Spanish, French, and English as well as his native German, who was not only a respected writer and intellectual but good-looking as well. His interest in me and the baby seemed little short of miraculous. I found miraculous, too, qualities in Bodo which were, especially for me then, appealingly the opposite of Jim's. Jim's impracticality and irresponsibility, apart from his writing, were traits I had previously easily identified with, even embraced, as being not unlike my own. But that was before the birth of the baby. Bodo was practical, reliable, and responsible—characteristics I was almost desperately in need of. And Bodo was not a talker, and though he was like Jim in being soft-spoken, he had a quieter nature that was refreshing—a sign of strength, I felt.

I saw Bodo as a way out—and aware of his attraction to me, I was able to fool myself and him into thinking I was in love—he fitted so perfectly everything I needed and wanted at that time, not the least because of his interest in and fondness for my one-year-old child. In a letter which Bodo wrote at that time to a friend living in Paris, he referred to Joel as the "delight and joy of my life," adding his wish that he would soon be able to adopt and care for him as his own.

In a little less than six weeks, Bodo and I were sleeping together and I had convinced both him and me that I was in love—convinced myself despite a vague awareness that I didn't really like sex with Bodo. As for Bodo, he was in love—besides which his loneliness as an exile made my ready-made family especially attractive. I was happy and hopeful, but not yet ready to tell Jim. Then Helen confided that she had already written and told Jim of my involvement. I don't remember minding. For a while the three of us, usually with the baby, went around Mexico City together, but after Bodo and I, with Joel, moved into an apartment in Mexico City, I thought of and saw Helen less and less—something she had every reason to resent.

On our first night in our apartment, Bodo and I stayed up talking until dawn, telling each other of our previous lives and loves, of ourselves and our dreams. I remember feeling proud that Bodo knew of Jim and admired his writing. It was during that night that I learned some of Bodo's political past, but I was at first mainly interested in his story of Ellen, the woman he loved and had lived with for six years. He gave her up without a word at the end of that time, still loving her, and she him, in order for each to honor a commitment made six years previously, when her lover had been sentenced to a six-year prison term for a political "crime." It was difficult for me to believe such integrity—if integrity it was. Then he showed me a picture of Ellen. I had somehow expected something glorious and glamorous, but looking out of the snapshot was a quiet-seeming, somewhat plain-looking woman with glasses. I remember feeling startled, and I realize now to what extent I was influenced by conventional good looks. I know that I relied on my own good looks to balance out my weak self-confidence and self-esteem, so that I probably gave good looks in others a disproportionate importance. And perhaps it is true that one searches for those attributes in another which one prizes in oneself.

Bodo also told me of the year and a half he had spent in Spain as a political commissar, during the Spanish Civil War, and how he had learned Yiddish commanding a Polish battalion. He said that the many nights he had spent awake in Spain, afraid to let himself sleep, had made him an exceptionally light sleeper. He had learned to speak Spanish in Spain, and I could hear the nostalgia with which he spoke of that time. He told of the good friends he had lost there, and seemed to have ambivalent feelings about coming out of Spain unhurt.

He showed me a snapshot which one of his comrades had taken of him interrogating two Spanish pilots who had been shot down. "What happened to them?" I asked. "They were fascists," Bodo said. "They were executed soon afterward." I was shocked—his words were so matter-of-fact, they were said so casually. But I said nothing—I didn't feel then like judging either Bodo or the deed.

From his suitcase he took out his latest book, *Leutnant Bertram,* and told me he had heard it was very popular among German prisoners of war in the United States. "Too bad I don't read German," I said. "I'd like to read it."

"Well, you can read it in English soon," he said. "It will be translated." Then he told me what it was about, and that it was based on his own life. I was shocked, because the hero of the book had been a Nazi. And that was how I learned that Bodo, some time in the late twenties, had joined the National Socialist party, the Nazis. A young poet and idealist, he had then believed in National Socialism as a solution to the grim aftermath of the Versailles Treaty, at the end of the First World War. Bodo had met Hitler and Goebbels then, and he was made editor of the only Nazi paper in the north of Germany. He went on to tell me that at that time he was living with a Jewish woman, the daughter of an American diplomat. When the Nazis asked him to publish an anti-Semitic article in his paper, he refused and soon thereafter went underground and made contact with the Communists. When Hitler came to power in 1933, Bodo, of course, was high on the Nazis' blacklist, and he knew he would be shot, if not worse, if he were caught. For months he lived from house to house, scarcely sleeping at all, until friends provided him with falsified papers to escape Germany and he was told of other friends he could approach in France. He described how he left, in early spring, with nothing except the clothes on his back, some money, and the precious papers. He was on foot, following one of the two routes his comrades had provided, and was not far from the Swiss border when a German guard-officer stopped him and asked for his passport. The guard, after a lengthy scrutiny of the papers, searched Bodo for weapons and told him he was under arrest. Both of them moved through the woods toward the officer's barracks some distance ahead. They walked on silently together, and Bodo told me how he was so sure his life was over that his thoughts were racing back to his early childhood, to his father—the proud German officer who had early given up on ever making a successful horseman and officer out of his young son—and he thought of the stepmother who reared him and his three brothers, and of all of Germany, his beloved country that he would never see again. They passed an old castle, abandoned and in ruins, not far from the road. Bodo told how he glanced up at the high turret of the castle and, scarcely believing his wish would be granted, asked the guard if he would allow him a few minutes to climb up there for a last look at Germany and the spring country-side. The guard consented—with the warning that he would be shot on the spot if he made any attempt to escape. But the guard also knew that Bodo was unarmed and that there was no other entry or exit from the castle. So Bodo climbed to the top, and after about ten minutes came down to resume his last few steps of freedom. He found the guard gone, and on the bottom step, near the entrance, were his papers. As Bodo ended his story I thought of how often I had heard the words "The only good German is a dead German," and I looked at Bodo and thought of the Nazi guard, realizing the falseness of any generalization about either a race or a nation.

By then it was almost three in the morning, and we passed into the kitchen to brew some coffee. I wanted to hear more, however, and he went on to tell me how, in France, he had written anti-Nazi material, pamphlets to be smuggled into Nazi Germany. It was there, too, that he wrote his first book, *Söldner und Soldat,* an account of his involvement with the Nazis and his eventual conversion to the communist cause. He joined the Communist party in Paris, and soon afterward, went to Spain as a political commissar—with other antifascist Germans in the war against Franco. After the defeat he returned to France, where he wrote his first novel, *Leutnant Bertram.* Bodo told me then that it was Dorothy Thompson, a well-known American journalist, who got him out of France, but I have since heard that it was Erica Mann, of the Thomas Mann family, who was most influential in getting him to the United States, where he stayed with the movie director Fritz Lang before going down to Mexico in 1940 to join other antifascists. President Cardenas of Mexico was then openly sympathetic and receptive to European anti-Nazis.

It was dawn when Bodo and I finally decided we should get some sleep because Joel could be counted on to be awake in a few hours.

Not long after that night, I was to meet Bodo's friends, primarily the Czech and German émigrés. They were a particularly close-knit group, mainly involved in running a German-language newspaper, *Neues Deutsch-land* (New Germany). They raised money to that end, as well as for the anti-fascist causes in general. They were Communists—tough, single-minded, and it seemed to me, amazingly selfless. I was impressed especially because of the vast difference I felt between them and the American Communists I had either known or known of. They too were single-minded and dedicated, and the American Communist party was probably never stronger or more zealous than during the thirties, at the height of the depression, with poverty and unemployment at all-time highs. But there was a political sophistication among the European Communists that I was aware of even while not fully understanding it. Perhaps it was the closeness of European borders which contributed to their knowledge of other cultures and languages. They all spoke at least one language besides their native tongue. And their dedication was based on harsh experience of a nature the American Communists had only heard described: they came from a Nazi-ridden country, some had served time for political "crimes," or had been in concentration camps either under Hitler or in France, after the fall of Loyalist Spain, when the French government treated the defeated antifascists almost as harshly as the Nazis did. These men and women were schooled and trained in a discipline un-known to Americans, simply because they had suffered under fascism and felt that socialism was the only way to avoid destruction, not only of themselves, but of the world.

I was also impressed by the apparent solidity of their marriages, and noticed that most of the women were exceedingly plain. There was no such solidity in marriages I knew of; besides, I had always thought that women, to be married at all, must be reasonably attractive.

One of the first of Bodo's friends I met was Egon Erwin Kisch, the Czech writer and journalist, and his wife, Gisl. Warm, simple, homely Gisl—one always felt her something of an afterthought next to Egon's bright wit, liveli-ness, charm, and talent for storytelling. But without Gisl, the continuous open-house atmosphere of their modest apartment in the Colonia Roma sec-tion of Mexico City could not have existed. Gisl, invariably modest and smil-ing, was the maker of coffee, continuously and every day, for the scores of guests who dropped in to hear the latest gossip or stories from Egon, the master storyteller, to drink a cup of coffee, or simply because they were wel-come there. And Gisl was more than the maker of coffee, for when guests were not around, she was typing and correcting Egon's manuscripts and editing his material, and when they were out of money, she was working as anyone's typist. And after Egon's death some years later in Czechoslovakia, Gisl spent her own remaining years gathering together Egon's manuscripts to preserve his memory. It is you too, Gisl, whose memory and worth should be honored and preserved.

But Egon Kisch was very special—and he was, together with Anna Seghers and Bodo Uhse, the main draw for fund-raising evenings. The group had almost no money, and the production of *Neues Deutschland,* from the writing of the articles to the printing and distribution, was the joint effort of all. My own part consisted of stuffing envelopes and distributing announcements around the city for upcoming events. The raising of money was as serious as running the paper itself. I remember the fund-raising events as both entertaining and interesting. The best-known of the writers either read from their works or simply spoke, with Anna Seghers' and Egon's evenings being the most entertaining and best attended.

Anna Seghers' book *The Seventh Cross* was already written when she arrived in Mexico from France. Her Hungarian husband, Rodi, and her two children, Ruth and Peter, came later. Anna's arrival was typical for refugees from Europe. Before someone landed, there was a general convening and scouting-around for the necessities to begin life in the city, and those already settled worked together to that end. A place to live had to be found and the rent paid, and everyone contributed whatever it was possible to find or give up in the way of furniture and general living needs. Then, later, as the person or family became settled and more or less on their own, there was a reshuffling and goods were returned or waited for the next arrival. I had never before experienced the kind of natural support and sense of togetherness I encountered in that group. But I was somewhat disappointed after Anna was settled and had become quite well-off. *The Seventh Cross,* translated into English and in line for a Hollywood movie, was paying large royalties, but my precious Big Ben alarm clock was not returned. The alarm clock, along with other contributions, had found its way to Anna's little apartment soon after her arrival. My Big Ben was important to me. It was not just an alarm clock, but a solid, shining chrome clock, distinctly American, with the special feature of "first it whispers, then it shouts," in contrast to the continuous jarring sound of the tinny Mexican timepiece I had purchased to take its place. Anna's answer, when Bodo eventually asked for my clock's return, rankled: "But now that you have a clock, you don't need this one any longer, do you?"

Nevertheless, Anna and I came to like each other more and more, though I now believe that she, like all Bodo's friends, must have been startled, certainly at first, by my political naïveté. I can still see Anna and hear her—her way of speaking, the words low, drawled out, distinct, and very powerful. Her white hair was pulled back carelessly from her face to form a kind of bun behind her head, never neat, and her humorous eyes were constantly blinking and squinting. She was, in fact, utterly charming, and it was all there twenty years later during the afternoon I spent with her in Berlin, when she was well past seventy years.

The German-speaking émigrés, apart from their meetings, fund-raising events, and newspaper, had a cultural club, the Heinrich Heine Club, which provided an opportunity for get-togethers, the production of plays, readings, and the like—all, of course, in German. Always invited to events at the Heinrich Heine Club were the bourgeois members of the German community— the bourgeois members as distinguished from the Communists. The bourgeois were also antifascists, mainly refugees from Hitler's Germany and occupied Europe, with no intention, however, of returning to Europe—unlike the Communists, who had no intention of remaining in Mexico once Hitler was defeated. The bourgeois refugees went into business almost immediately on arrival in Mexico, almost before they had learned Spanish, and they stood, for me, in sharp contrast to the political refugees, whose main goal was the furtherance of their cause and the defeat of Hitler and fascism. The bourgeois were educated and cultured and found in the Communists a needed escape from their own boredom with themselves, and for some, even with Mexico. They also, aside from making up a large membership in the Heinrich Heine Club, gave generously toward events, turned up regularly at those events, and were friends and guests of the more lively and interesting of the political émigrés—Egon Erwin Kisch, Bodo, Anna Seghers, Kurt Stern and his French wife, Jeanne, and André Simone (Otto Katz), who some years later would be hanged by the Czech government for "imperialist crimes."

I don't remember talk among Bodo's friends about the Hitler-Stalin Nonaggression Pact during the first months I was in Mexico, though I was aware that many thousands of Communists all over the world had left the party, disillusioned and bitter, when Stalin made the agreement with Hitler. I remember clearly, however, when I first heard that Germany had attacked the Soviet Union. Bodo and I were standing talking with some friends on a Mexico City street. Bodo must have received the news shortly before; as he was telling of the attack, he began to seem taller to me, clearer, and more alive.

His relief was evident enough for me to realize the burden the pact must have been to him—whatever the party had said in explanation. But now Bodo could hold up his head—it had all been a ploy, and Stalin, clever Stalin, had known all along that Hitler would break the agreement, that Germany would attack the Soviet Union. The pact was merely to buy time, to gather strength for the attack Stalin knew was coming.

Most of the households of the German émigrés had a large map pasted or pinned to the wall, telling of the progress of the war, the advances and retreats made clear with little pins with round red (for the Red army) or blue heads. And when the tide began to turn against the Germans—when the red pins began to move toward the Soviet border, forcing the Nazis out and away from Stalingrad—there was a clear intensification of excitement and hope.

Pablo Neruda and his wife, Delia, were in Mexico then. The Chilean government, aware of the power and influence Neruda exercised, had sent him to Mexico as ambassador, with Enrique Delano as cultural attaché. Both, as Communists, were immediately friends with the German émigrés, as was José Herrera Petére, a handsome blond poet whose brother had recently been killed in Spain. I loved Petére, who to me was particularly beautiful with his blond hair and expressive blue eyes. I remember feeling embarrassment and even pain just looking at him. Perhaps I was in love with him. Petére played the guitar, and knew all the Spanish songs of the international brigades, and we played them together, Petére singing and playing his guitar and I improvising on the violin. It was a good combination, and I looked forward to our sessions together. The last time I remember seeing Petére was when we met accidentally on a street in Mexico City. He was taking home a birthday present he had just bought for his young son, and he unpacked it to show me. It was a miniature mouth organ, and as he held it for me to see, his eyes showed a terrible fear of failure and pain and doubt—all saying so clearly, Did I choose right? Will he like it? It's so poor—and I could feel in myself a wonder, something like heartbreak. Petére never knew how I felt or what I thought I saw in him, nor did anyone else, for that matter. Over the years I have occasionally spoken of a Spanish poet I knew in Mexico, a blond, handsome young poet, a good poet they told me, and very lovable.

Neruda's wife, Delia, a good-looking, blond Argentine woman, was twenty-five years older than he. Like so many other wives I knew then, she was devoted and attentive. She too served coffee, at all times of the day, and it was not unusual for Pablo to come home to their Mexico City house with some fifteen or twenty friends in tow. On one such occasion, I remember approaching with fascination the Nerudas' pet anteater, who, less friendly then he appeared, bit me severely. There were some fifteen of us on that occasion, and it was Delia's role to serve up whatever there was for the entire entourage, during which Pablo "held court," a role I remember him in, not only in Mexico, but later in Berlin, where we, along with other friends, usually visited him and Delia in his hotel room. There, surrounded by admirers, Pablo sometimes recited his wonderful poems—always in a loud, sonorous, and affected voice. Delia, by then showing the large difference in ages, was trying to "keep up" with makeup, jewels, and high heels. It was during one of the hotel-room meetings that I met Pablo's great love, Matilde—a Chilean, handsome, redheaded, and a poet in her own right. Delia was also there then, and I was unaware of any significance in Matilde's presence. When we heard, not too long afterward, that Pablo was leaving Delia for Matilde, it was easy to come down on the side of Delia, Pablo's wife of so many years and now, so very much older, discarded for the younger woman. Pablo, I remember, was almost universally condemned, and I too, having known and liked Delia, felt strongly for her. Pablo, however, who was only fifty at the time, had fallen fully in love, and he wrote some of his best poems to Matilde. I found it then, and still find it, hard and unfair to judge him. The last I heard of Delia, she had gone to live out her life in Paris.

Dear Pablo. How shy and inadequate I always felt in his presence, and how pleased I was in the knowledge of his liking me despite my inadequacies, or more accurately, my foolishness. I did feel stupid around him, except for the time, in Berlin during a gathering at some club or other, that I drank enough to call out to him, on a sudden impulse, "Pablo! I love you!" and he responded by dancing with me. I felt one of those rare and wonderful physical attractions, and I knew it was mutual, so for almost a month, or until he left Berlin, I felt in love and was even more shy and tongue-tied in his presence.

Years later, back in New York, intent on a new and other life, with Bodo dead and my years in Mexico and, subsequently, Germany behind me, I found myself walking through the Village and up Seventh Avenue, and seeing, but not recognizing, Pablo Neruda coming toward me. He was, as always, heading a small entourage, and as we approached, he recognized me first, because this Pablo was thin, aged, and sickly. But yes, it was Pablo, and we ran toward each other to embrace in the Mexican fashion and mumble words of joy at the unexpected meeting and of sorrow over Bodo's death. Some two years after that chance encounter, I heard of Pablo's end—was it cancer or murder?—back in his beloved Chile.

Like almost everyone living in Mexico except, of course, the very poor, we had a maid, a *criada:* Guadalupe, or Zita, as we called her. She lived, as did other *criadas,* in one of the small rooms provided for servants on the rooftop of the apartment house. Also on the rooftop were the concrete tubs for washing and the lines for hanging out clothes. Washing machines were unheard of, and unheard of too was anyone except a *criada* doing the wash. In Mexico, where labor is the cheapest commodity, the more than full-time work of the *criada* is taken for granted—I put that purposely in the present tense because I don't believe there has been much change since the forties, certainly not outside Mexico City. Zita's life was typical of the vast majority of Mexican women then. When she came to us, she was twenty-three and married to Federico, who shared her little room on the roof. Zita was a full-blooded Oaxacan Indian, handsome, with wonderful slanted eyes, brown skin, and a strong body. Her body had to be strong: at thirteen she had come alone from Oaxaca to Mexico City and gone to work at a small hotel washing sheets by hand. That was about the time she began to menstruate, and she told me how the hotel guests, anxious to get their money's worth, or perhaps merely thoughtless, cleaned their shoes on the sheets—which, of course, she had to rub clean against the cement washboards. Zita was happy to work for an American. Americans always paid more than the usual monthly wage of thirty pesos. And I was happy to have Zita, who over the years turned out to be more a beloved sister than a servant. Despite (or perhaps because of) the fact that she could neither read nor write, she was, I soon realized, exceptionally sharp-witted and highly intelligent. Naturally there was a vast difference in culture, but there were genuine understanding and trust and love between us, and she adored Joel. I know it was Zita rather than Bodo or I who brought Joel up during our years in Mexico City. Zita, with her heavy-lidded, slanting eyes, her quick mind and loving nature—I have thought of her so often through the years, wanting to know where she is, and if she is still alive. Zita and I wanted to stay together, and to that end we both once spent many hours trying to overcome her illiteracy problem. It was a problem because any exit permit, or visa to enter another country, was obtainable only if she could read and write. I was appalled at the enormous difficulty she had simply learning to hold a pencil—so simple an act for anyone accustomed from childhood to writing. Learning to read was somewhat easier—she had taught herself a little, watching subtitles at the movies. But neither of us counted on the sort of book she was given when we went to secure the necessary papers—I don't remember the title or even the contents, but it was a book complicated enough to ensure that only the highly educated would pass the test. Of course, she failed. After I left Mexico, I made attempts to write to Zita, but I gave them up after a year. Nor did I receive word either from or about her. When I returned to Mexico some years after we had left, I tried to find her, looking through endless records and telephone books, questioning officials, and knowing, even as I tried, that it was hopeless and that I would never know what had become of her. For Zita was just one among millions of illiterate women, helpless *criadas,* women without rights or protection.

We left Joel with Zita the time we drove with Egon Kisch and Gisl to see the newly erupted volcano, Parícutin. It was one of the rare times that we went anywhere outside Mexico City. And it turned out to be fun traveling with Egon. He had by then become something of an authority on Mexico—knew the places of special interest, where, for instance, every remote and little known Orozco fresco could be found. Exactly a year before, he had traveled to the volcano, when it had first rumbled and burst through the earth. I soon found myself wishing, however, that Egon hadn't already witnessed it, for at possibly the most enthralling and momentous moment of my life, when Bodo and I were standing silent and in complete awe at the rhythmic billowing and belching of great rocks and lava high into the gray, soot-filled air, and were tightly holding hands in near disbelief at what we were witnessing and hearing, Egon, moving up behind us, spoke. "This is nothing," he said, and described how much more awesome and inspiring and terrifying it had been during his first visit a year previously. I didn't know, and still do not, whether to be disgusted or simply to find it very funny that some American tourists threw a birthday cake, complete with one lighted candle, down into the vast retching cavity that day.

Bodo and I had been living together about a year and a half, and I wanted a divorce from Jim badly. Naturally I had been asking for one in my letters to him, and though my requests were never directly refused, neither were they granted. My letters also told Jim something of my life and Joel's development, and occasionally Jim sent down money for the three of us, as did my father. I was never concerned, as Bodo was, about the problem of money. My needs were relatively small, besides which I was accustomed to being taken care of, and was sure everything would work out all right. Bodo, more practical than

I, was aware that the small amount he received from the Anti-Fascist League of Writers would be far from adequate for the three of us. Nevertheless, I wanted a divorce and I wanted to marry Bodo, nor did my thinking go much beyond that wish. A trip to New York and a direct confrontation seemed the only way. I was also missing my violin, and wanted my recordings with me in Mexico. I still had the Chevy my father had given me when Helen and I left New York, and the journey back, it was decided, would be paid for by the passengers I would get. One of them turned out to be Lupe Marin, the first wife of Diego Rivera.

Lupe was a tall, handsome Mexican woman, with long dark hair and brown eyes. I remember her telling me that she was forty years old, and since I was ten years younger, she seemed really old to me. Lupe planned to be in New York just long enough to appear at a trial. Someone had written a biography of Diego Rivera and had intimated, or perhaps said directly, that Lupe and Diego had never married, thus illegitimating her two daughters. Lupe was suing for a hundred thousand dollars.

The other women passengers I scarcely remember, except that miles of pine forest in Maine were owned by one of them, the purpose of whose trip was the establishment of that ownership. I have a less pleasant memory of the third passenger, a young southern woman whose patronizing views and comments on Negroes put me on edge almost from the start of our trip. I realized almost immediately that I had chosen badly, and done an equally bad job of calculating the expense of driving to New York. Of the three women, none could drive, so that I was the sole driver for some three thousand miles. I soon also found that I had to translate menus and find toilets throughout the trip—at first for the two Americans, since they spoke no Spanish, and then, after crossing the border, for Lupe Marin, who spoke no English. Happily, the southern woman went only as far as Laredo and I was spared her company and a possible quarrel during the drive through the southern states. What she thought of me I do not know, but I think we were both aware of a mutual hostility.

In New York, as soon as I reached my room after checking in at a hotel, I called Jim. Twenty minutes later he was there, smiling a cracked, painful smile as he held out a little bunch of flowers. I knew immediately that he was still in love with me, but that did not affect me apart from boosting my ego and self-confidence. The ten days in New York were relatively uneventful—visits with Jim were mainly made up of unsuccessful efforts to secure a divorce. I met with friends I had known, and had a short meeting with the photographer Robert Capa at a bar, where he gave me a suitcase of his clothes for Bodo. Bodo had known Capa in Spain; they liked each other, and the friendship was renewed in Mexico, where they had been mainly drinking companions at the Hotel Montejo when Capa was there in 1940. As soon as I met the photographer in New York, I understood why Bodo liked him so much, and I understood too the exchange of clothes. Capa's build and height were almost identical to Bodo's, and a quick glance at Capa's elegant tweed jacket told me that the suitcase he had given me was likely stuffed with "goodies." I was charmed by him, and I felt he knew it, or perhaps was accustomed to having people find him charming. It didn't matter, though, probably because I detected no arrogance, but saw only a strongly intelligent face with a ready, wide-mouthed smile and dark, flashing eyes. He clearly cared about Bodo and was interested in anything I had to tell of the life Bodo and I shared in Mexico. We both had to leave after a single drink taken on high stools before a bar. Then, with the suitcase for Bodo on the floor behind us, Capa paid the bill, we shook hands, smiling into each other's eyes, and he left. But when I turned around, the precious consignment was gone—picked up and carried off by someone probably just minutes before. I don't like to remember Bodo's disappointment when, back in Mexico, I told him of the loss.

Lupe Marin was my only passenger on the drive back. She had won her case, with an award, however, of only a token penny. Her humiliation and fury were evident all the way home in the abrupt change in her attitude toward America and everything American, an attitude which during the drive up to New York had been open and friendly. On the return journey, her bitterness and bias were sometimes difficult to bear. Shortly before we reached the border, we spent our last night in the United States at a motel. Lupe decided she liked, and wanted to possess one of, the little lamps on either side of the twin beds. I felt that her wanting it was part of her new prejudice against America, but I said nothing except that if she wanted it badly enough, she should take it; it would fit into her suitcase, and it probably wouldn't be missed, or if it was, it certainly wasn't worth much. She thought about it and then asked me to take it for her. "Why?" I said. "I don't want it. I don't even like it." Her strange response was, "But you're the communist here, aren't you? After all, you're living with a well-known Communist. Equal distribution—isn't that what it's all about?" Neither of us took the lamp.

We arrived at the border a few months after the United States had declared war on Germany. By some fluke the lock to the car trunk had become packed with mud, and we were unable to open it for customs. The border guards did not believe this was accidental, and it was soon evident that their mistrust was also based on a detailed personal dossier on me. A drill was procured, the trunk opened, and then began what turned out to be more than four hours of interrogation, including a session with a woman guard who led me to a small cubicle and ordered me to undress. Her careful examination of my clothes and person was accomplished deadpan, with no response to my questioning with either a smile or a word. They had all become convinced, on seeing the trunk full of books and classical recordings, that I was truly dangerous, another Mata Hari perhaps. Two other guards began to go through the books, page by page. There were two cartons of books, and the guards soon became bored. At a battered windup phonograph, I saw one serious lanky young man bent over, listening carefully to a recording of the Brahms Fourth Symphony, obviously hoping for some juicy secret message. Then one of the guards, going through the luggage, was pleased to come up with a short note I had tucked back into it carelessly. It was from Bodo, penciled on the back of a flyer from the Heinrich Heine Club; the note began, "Liebes Mädchen . . ." That did it—it was in German, and to those border guards, all Germans, Nazis or antifascists, were the same, and enemies. They were also obviously disgusted with my personal life: legally married to an American, but living out of wedlock with a German in Mexico, a German with whom I had left my American child. If I wasn't a spy, my personal life made me as bad.

Lupe Marin, meanwhile, was in a state of complete fury, stamping back and forth screaming, "Yo protesto!" and, of course, seeing it all as unnecessary harassment by those Americans.

Eventually we were allowed to proceed into Mexico, with the books, recordings, and general belongings. I think the guards became tired of Lupe and me, and possibly disappointed too. They had found no tangible evidence. We drove on, and I learned soon afterward that the border guards were no longer allowing books and recordings through: such suspect material was kept and sent to its owners much later.

Back with Bodo in Mexico, I realized what an exceptional father he was to Joel. That was brought home to me very particularly as I observed the closeness that had developed between them. Bodo also had, despite our lack of money, bought an expensive wool blanket for Joel, and I didn't know whether to be shocked by the extravagance or grateful for his thoughtfulness. I was especially gratified to see Bodo's pleasure over the records and books I had brought back. All in all, it was a good time between us, and I felt a strong bond—a new family closeness.

Some weeks later, Bodo and I, with two visiting American friends, May and Sam Brooks, went out for dinner and dancing at the Hotel Reforma. It was around one in the morning. The bill had been paid, and we were ready to leave but were still sitting at our table, waiting for Sam to return from the men's room. A tall, somewhat beefy-looking man—he looked American— was sitting and drinking alone at a nearby table. He called over—friendly, as Americans can be—and asked if we'd mind if he joined us. We were cordial, one of us adding that we were leaving soon. He came over anyway and sat down, a little drunk but friendly enough. We began to talk, the kind of talk common to people who share a language and country: "Where are you from?" and so on. He turned out to be from Texas, and I said something about how one could almost have guessed it. Bodo then said something equally harmless. The Texan suddenly turned to Bodo and, his voice dripping with suspicion, almost snarled, "Where'd you get that accent?" Bodo's reply, whatever it was to be, was lost as the Texan yelled, "You goddamn German," and half-rising from his chair, hit Bodo full in the face. Bodo, in an automatic move to avoid the blow, upset the chair. The commotion that followed alerted two or three Mexican waiters, who moved quickly to Bodo and stood over and around him protectively, one of them saying, "Don't worry. We're for Hitler, too." None of us got any sleep that night. Bodo and the aggressive Texan were both sent to jail. They were given a slap on the wrist by a judge the following morning, and then released.

5 *The Emigrants*

*A*merica was at war, but my involvement, or more correctly, my awareness, was mainly vicarious. I was not directly affected. I do have a sharp memory of the German blitzkrieg, and of a sense of amazement that the seemingly invincible Nazi army could overrun all of Europe by 1939 or 1940. Although I was Jewish, I do not remember feeling personally threatened, and even the vivid accounts in *Time* magazine of the Nazi government's attacks on the Jews, and of concentration camps, left them seeming remote. Perhaps I had a sense of impotence, but mainly, I believe, I saw the events as happening in Europe, to other people, so that the effect was not unlike what I felt in reading of a murder or atrocity in a sensationalist newspaper. All this had nothing to do with me or those I knew and loved—my own life was safe. I reacted the same way some years later, when the people of Hiroshima suffered the explosion of the atom bomb. My closeness to the German émigrés did give me more political awareness than I would otherwise have had, but it was not until I was in Germany, seeing evidence and reading of Hiroshima, watching movies and visiting the Buchenwald concentration camp, that I realized the horror of Hiroshima, or the awful extent of the Nazi crimes.

It may seem strange that during so many years of my life, I, who have never been a political person, was as close as I was to left-thinking people and fully committed communists. It is less strange, though, in light of the way I have always been drawn to the underprivileged and the helpless. That was the basis for the sympathy I felt with people whose politics were motivated by outrage at injustices. Nor should one forget the general climate of the thirties—the years of the Great Depression, Roosevelt's New Deal, and the young Soviet Union, which was still giving hope to many. It was a time when it was fashionable to be on the Left, and when leftist thinking and human intelligence were practically synonymous.

It may also be surprising that a Jewish-American woman would choose to live in East Germany. One would naturally think that this must have been motivated by a strong political commitment. I know, however, that my reasons were mainly personal, given that I had both a tendency to move forward rather than to remain still and an adventurous streak that inevitably led me to take chances and to adapt to the many accidents which came my way, much as a trickle of water changes its direction according to the contours of its surroundings.

After almost two years of living in Mexico City, Bodo and I decided to move to Cuernavaca, an hour or so away. Cuernavaca would be cheaper, and Bodo could write quietly and commute once a week to Mexico City for his other pursuits. And I had only Joel to care for. We soon found a house more than suitable, a relative mansion even for our few available dollars. It was on a hill above the town, which in those days was not the sprawling and corrupt city it has become. The three bedrooms each had a wash basin, without, however, a more necessary clothes closet. The bathroom, all in black tile, had a tub sunk so low that cleaning it was possible only by climbing down in. A rectangular hallway had, at each end, five steps leading down to an enormous solarium, round, all glass, and rising to a dome some twenty feet above. The perimeter, of course, was filled with soil for plants, and the solarium floor was covered with the usual pretty tile common to many Mexican houses. Elegant as the house was, or certainly had once been, the kitchen was abysmal. It was set far enough away from the house to necessitate, during the rainy season, an umbrella to bring dishes back and forth. There was no stove, only a crude *bracero*, a small charcoal-burning oven, and nothing else of cooking importance. It almost seemed as though some thought had gone into that kitchen to make it as thoroughly disagreeable, inconvenient, and inaccessible as possible. It was clearly meant for that lowest and most despised creature, the Mexican *criada*.

The grounds around the house were magnificent, especially the swimming pool: full-sized and surrounded by bougainvillea and banana trees. On one side of the house was a smaller pool, and a half dozen grapefruit trees, the whole surrounded by a high iron fence. We paid a hundred pesos a month, or the equivalent of twenty dollars. We had no water, but that was eventually remedied, and I do not remember later paying a higher rent. It was a strange and wonderful house, but not a happy one, as I was soon to discover.

Cuernavaca had much to offer. I loved the semitropical air, the quiet, lazy pace. Joel soon found a playmate, and I even liked the tourist atmosphere, feeling superior to it since I was actually living there. Neither Bodo nor I had anything to do with the American colony—they were, we knew, mainly well-to-do, politically conservative, and on the whole uninterested in and even unsympathetic with Mexican Indians. A disagreeable image comes to mind of a small group of drunken Americans who had bought a child's coffin, and thought it terribly funny to carry it aloft across the main square, or zocalo, receiving respects and condolences from the natives, until one of the Americans lurched, slipped, and fell, exposing the open, empty coffin to the disgust and fury of the onlookers.

I don't remember when I first met Dorothy—I don't think I ever knew her last name. She was a kind of permanent American tourist, somewhere in her thirties, who lived in a suite at the Hotel Bella Vista. I could find her sitting on the terrace of the hotel, drinking her highball. Her hand always trembled slightly as she lifted the whiskey to her mouth. It was pleasant to have her almost always there, to sit with her occasionally, gossip, and watch the endless parade of passersby: Indian women with baskets on their heads, the baskets laden with bright red tomatoes or luscious fruits; children selling Chiclets; families with children trailing along, and the tourists—the women usually dressed (as we both were) in the brightly colored blouses and flouncy skirts offered in almost every store window.

Dorothy was childless, still pretty, rich with alimony, and bored to apathy. She was less bored after she began sleeping with Miguel. He was a lively, handsome young Mexican, only slightly corrupted by the tourist atmosphere of Cuernavaca, who made his living with his guitar on the terraces of the hotels, playing and singing for the guests and passersby. Dorothy wasn't exactly in love with him; she didn't even trust him. In fact, some weeks before, when local gossip was at its height after the attack and robbery of two American women tourists, Dorothy told me how she had prudently placed her jewels in a safety deposit vault in one of the town's banks. But she liked Miguel well enough, and he certainly relieved some of the dullness of her life. True, she read books, even good ones, and she painted. But when I knew her, she scarcely touched her paintbrushes, though I remember once in her apartment seeing her easel still standing and displaying her last effort—a large portrait in oil, surprisingly well executed, of a seated woman, a friend who, like Dorothy, was whiling away her time and life in Cuernavaca.

Dorothy first told me of her idea some four months after she had begun sleeping with Miguel. Miguel was married, and sometimes, on the way to the marketplace, his wife, Guadalupe, passed the hotel veranda where Miguel and Dorothy, and sometimes I, sat. Guadalupe was a beautiful, full-blooded Indian girl of eighteen. She already had two small children and was now big with her third. And it was this, Guadalupe's coming child, that lay at the heart of Dorothy's idea.

We both watched her often, singling her out from among the other native women who thronged the squares and marketplaces—her worn pink-and-green-striped straw market basket in one hand, in the other the small hand of the three-year-old, who trotted patiently beside her, and the littlest one, his black eyes bright and inquiring, peering out of her faded, blue rebozo, just above her bulging belly. Guadalupe always looked straight ahead as she walked, and her two thick black braids, plaited with bits of bright pink wool, reached below her waist.

It was hard to tell what Dorothy felt about Guadalupe. We both knew that Miguel went home sometimes during the week, to leave a few pesos for her tortillas and frijoles, to sleep with her on the straw petate in a corner of their hut, and to listen to the street gossip and tales of the children. Certainly it never occurred to her that Miguel really loved his wife. I believe that Miguel was less interested in her than Dorothy was.

Sometimes Dorothy, dressed in one of her bright skirts and peasant blouses, would cross the sun-flooded village square and make her way up one of the narrow little streets to Lupe's hut, to talk with her and give her friendly advice on child care and hygiene. I imagine that Lupe, on these occasions, listened with the politeness instinctive to her race. She rarely spoke, Dorothy told me. Dorothy never knew what was behind the long, almond-shaped, tilted Indian eyes—they seemed so utterly without expression. But beautiful she was, Dorothy readily conceded, only so hopelessly ignorant that she didn't even know how to read or write, and now in that wretched little hut she was going to give birth again, on the petate, of course, and the children would be there. Dorothy resented the children.

It must have been during one of these visits that Dorothy's idea took root, the idea that Lupe would have her baby in a real bed, on a real mattress, with clean white sheets, in a room with curtained windows, and a licensed doctor in attendance. Dorothy would make all this possible. I was intrigued when she told me of her plan.

Dorothy was no longer bored. She spent sleepless nights happily searching out and examining each last detail of her project. Her main concern, as she confided to me, was Miguel's approval. Lupe, she believed, would consent only if her husband ordered her. But Dorothy need not have worried. I told Miguel, who readily agreed. He was, in fact, scarcely interested—a little mystified, perhaps, and of course amused. As for his wife, he told me that Dorothy scarcely existed for her, that Lupe's jealousy, ferocious as it could be, did not embrace *la gringa*. I kept to myself some of my talk with Miguel. Dorothy went ahead with her plans, and for the next few weeks I hardly saw her.

Then one day, late in the afternoon, Dorothy telephoned, and her voice was husky and excited through the wire. "The baby's on the way—if you want to see a birth, you'd better come quick!" That it was going to be a show was new to me. Did I want to see a birth? I had never thought about it before, nor did I think then. I simply went, out the gate and down our little street toward the main square and Dorothy's apartment. It was almost dusk. The colored adobe fronts of the houses glowed soft in the fading sunlight, pink, pale green, blue, white, and a small knot of tired looking burros stood patiently with hanging ears before the cantina on the corner. The square was almost empty of people. Only the two main hotels had their usual quota of tourists on the balconies and terraces, playing dominoes or rummy, drinking iced daiquiris and Martinis before supper. A small group of mariachis, their broad sombreros low over dark, serious faces, were playing and singing for some of them: "Yo no te ofrezco riquezas, te ofrezco mi corazón, te ofrezco mi corazón en cambio de mi pobreza . . ." ("I do not offer you riches, I offer you my heart, I offer you my heart in exchange for my poverty . . .").

The door to Dorothy's apartment was ajar when I arrived. I passed through and found her standing in the foyer by the telephone. She jerked her head in the direction of a closed door behind her. "She's in there. Go on in if you want." Dorothy was almost completely drunk and trembling with hysteria. "The goddamn doctor still hasn't turned up—been calling all over town for hours." From behind the closed door there was no sound, but from the patio below there came a terrible, persistent wailing, the tired, desperate wail of an exhausted, frightened child, or was it two? "That's been going on for hours, too—her two brats!—no wonder I'm a wreck!" It would be almost dark by now, down in the patio, but Dorothy's idea had centered on Lupe, not her children.

The room where Lupe was about to give birth was beautiful. It was, in fact, Dorothy's own spacious living room, converted for the occasion. And everything was there, just as she had planned. Soft pale yellow curtains were drawn across the two broad windows on either side of the bed. The bed itself, normally Dorothy's own, was an immense carved-oak four-poster affair, an exact copy of the bed of Hernando Cortés, complete with the small carved wooden steps beside it. In one corner of the room, standing against the wall, was the waiting bassinet, a mass of embroidery and delicate soft white muslin ruffles, the whole outrageously elaborate, ridiculous, and pathetic.

Lupe's beautiful dark Indian face was turned toward the other wall. Her heavy braids, mussed and partly unplaited, lay softly black against the creamy white woolen blanket which covered her distended belly. Even before her eyes met mine, I was sorry I had entered, but the eyes were terrible. I was a stranger. And then her long brown hands clenched into tight fists as the pains began again.

Down in the patio the little three-year-old, his own face grimy and smeared with tears, was wiping the streaming nose of his tiny brother. I led them, whimpering and sniffling, up to the lighted apartment where Dorothy, haggard with distress and utterly helpless, was sitting limply before the telephone, a glass of whiskey in her hand. At the sight of the children she came to life. "What the hell am I supposed to do with them now—isn't the place messed up enough as it is?" But Lupe's voice came through the closed door, calling the names of her children.

I got them in, though Dorothy fought with all the strength she had left. Lupe's face, as I closed the door behind me, was strong and quiet. She would come through all right. Only, the bassinet—vaguely I wondered what would become of it when Lupe was back in her little hut with her three children.

Out in the street it was dark except for the faint glow of streetlamps and lighted windows. On the broad terrace of the Hotel Bella Vista a few tourists were sitting quietly, enjoying the mild evening air and listening to someone playing a guitar and singing. The voice was Miguel's. As I crossed the deserted square the face of a small boy loomed up out of the dark. "Buy a Chiclet, Señora, please . . . ?" I hurried past, and only minutes later did the pinched, desperate little face really register. I went on home.

My life with Bodo at that time centered mainly on Joel and on Bodo's closest friend, Alfred Miller, also German. I took their friendship for granted then, but thinking of it now, I see it as both wonderful and strange, mainly because of the enormous difference between them. Bodo was an intellectual and poet, introverted, extremely sensitive, even delicate. Alfred, on the other hand, was clearly blue-collar—a worker. Intelligent but not an intellectual, he had a face and body which were solid and tough; only his eyes, warm and brown, showed his sensitivity, warmth, and humanity. Alfred loved Bodo and seemed to understand him. What they had in common was their political beliefs—they were both dedicated Communists. Alfred was a correspondent for the *Daily Worker* in New York. He had spent some years during the late thirties organizing blacks and poor whites in the South of the United States—extremely dangerous work and a mark of both his courage and his dedication. Alfred was an orphan raised in poverty, without ever knowing who his mother and father were. And just as he never spoke of his years of organizing in the South, he rarely spoke of his early life in Germany, the years after World War I during which Käthe Kollwitz produced her famous drawings of unemployment and hunger, especially of women and children. Alfred invariably went off by himself on Christmas Eve—he was always then doggedly unavailable. It was only after his death that I learned that he spent those evenings wandering the streets of the poorer sections of Mexico City, distributing toys and food to children.

Despite Alfred's attachment to Bodo, he was, I knew, in love with me. Sometimes when he looked at me, I saw his eyes mist over. I pretended to be oblivious, however, and it never entered my head that the situation was potentially a dangerous one. I simply took secret pleasure in the knowledge of Alfred's attraction to me and the power that my unavailability gave me. And Alfred, because of his close friendship with Bodo, kept safely distant, never speaking of his feelings, and seemed to be unaware of my subtle flirting. He lived in Mexico City during that time and spent his weekends with Bodo and me in Cuernavaca. It was a pleasant period, and it was during one of those weekends that I had my thirtieth birthday. A few friends had come down from Mexico City to spend the day, but most memorable was the evening. Bodo sent me to town on some pretext, and while I was gone he and Alfred fashioned thirty little paper boats and placed a little candle in each of them. On my return, I was greeted with the fairy-tale sight of the boats floating on the silent water of the swimming pool.

During one of my occasional trips to Mexico City, some fluke made it impossible to return to Cuernavaca, as usual, the same day. I had to spend the night at Alfred's apartment. There, after a deadpan discussion about who should sleep on the floor, we decided it was silly to avoid sharing the bed, and the rest was inevitable. Inevitable not only because Bodo and I had never been at ease with each other sexually, but because Bodo had told Alfred of our difficulties. Sleeping with Alfred was a revelation. I had almost forgotten how good sex could be. And Alfred became even more drawn to me. For almost exactly one year after that night, Alfred and I met whenever possible, always careful to keep our secret from Bodo, who was very busy working on his novel, meeting regularly with the German group, and writing articles for the German newspaper. Alfred never discussed the sexual difficulties between Bodo and me, but asked me again and again to leave Bodo to marry him.

I never seriously considered that, and I believe the reasons are almost too complicated to unravel. For one thing, Bodo and I never so much as mentioned the possibility of separating, and I had come to view Bodo as Joel's father: certainly Bodo loved Joel as if he were his own son. He also loved me, and probably believed that any movement we made away from each other should originate with me. As for myself, I not only loved Bodo, but the sting of Jim's betrayal of me and Joel was still with me, so that, watching Bodo's devotion to Joel, I felt grateful, rewarded, and even proud that a man like Bodo was now Joel's father. I trusted him completely, and the knowledge of his love and trust made it too easy for me to find excuses to drive into Mexico City—to spend time with Alfred, to sink into his love and passion for me. It was so easy, and seemed so natural, that it hardly occurred to me that what I was doing was not only dangerous but utterly reprehensible. Nor can I come up, at this time, with any excuse other than my usual vagueness—a tendency not to look ahead, and to let things ride.

I have never understood why Bodo and I never felt right in sex together, and it seems somehow too easy to blame it on "chemistry." Perhaps, in the beginning, inexperienced as I was, and accustomed to Jim's sexual directness and even aggressiveness, I failed to understand Bodo's reserve and subtlety. I remember misinterpreting it as a lack of interest—I was used to being pursued. And Bodo, very likely, expecting more participation, probably concluded that I too wasn't that interested or was possibly even cold. I don't remember any open discussions—both because we were shy and because there wasn't as much openness in those years. At any rate, after what I experienced as an overly delicate clumsiness and lack of interest on Bodo's part, Alfred's rough manner seemed more like Jim, and I therefore felt more relaxed and at ease. I cared for, and appreciated Bodo, but I took him more and more for granted, and put far back in my mind any thought of future danger. Everything was going so well; even sex between Bodo and me seemed to be improving. There was no lessening of the strength of Bodo and Alfred's friendship when the three of us spent weekends together. There was genuine affection between us, and it seemed to me then like a perfect arrangement—with each of us having what we wanted. I preferred not to look too far below the surface—and I ignored the tension in Alfred and me created by the knowledge of Bodo's ignorance, and Alfred's and my guilt and discomfort in the betrayal.

Jim came to Cuernavaca that year. He had written saying he wanted to visit me and Joel: would it be all right, and could I get him a room at a hotel nearby? He would stay about a week. I can still see Bodo's face as I returned from picking Jim up at the airport that May morning. He is giving our German shepherd a bath in front of the house, and as Jim and I drive slowly past on our way to park the car, Bodo, bent over the soapy dog, turns a smiling face up in greeting, and Jim's words please me as he says, almost under his breath, "I like that guy." That night Bodo and Jim talked until three in the morning, and when Alfred arrived from Mexico City the following day, I was happy to see that Alfred and Jim liked each other as well. Jim, scheduled to remain for a week, remained over a month, staying at our house rather than in the hotel room I had arranged for him. I lived during that month as under a charm, and in full self-assuredness, knowing of the love of those three men. A little more than a year later I was to experience the loss of each of them, and I remember sensing my loss as three violent, almost simultaneous blows. My mood before that, however, was utterly confident. Jim, I knew, was still in love with me, and as Bodo confided one evening, he had asked Bodo if he would consent to my being in New York six months out of each year. I don't remember being consulted on that idea, which must have died soon after it was born.

Jim, unlike Bodo, was immediately aware that Alfred was in love with me. "What makes you so sure?" I asked, somewhat worried that he may have guessed more. "It's not hard to see," he answered. "He can hardly take his eyes off you." Bodo, however, astute though he was in every other area, noticed nothing. Jim and I went horseback riding sometimes—I remember once feeling something like triumph noticing his glance of admiration as I ran down the steps of our house to meet him. I was wearing a bright orange Mexican cowboy outfit—black cording down the sides of each tightly fitting trouser leg. Sometimes, during the evening, I listened to the three of them—Bodo, Alfred, and Jim endlessly discussing subjects which I didn't feel sufficiently informed about, or perhaps didn't feel interested enough in, to join the conversation—until I went off to bed, content in the knowledge of their friendship. I knew that Jim enjoyed helping me put Joel to bed evenings. His face then always glowed with love and interest in Joel, who by then was about three years old and as lovely as a child can be at that age. I had not forgotten, however, my last year with Jim, and the powerful sense of betrayal I had felt, so I buried any impulse toward compassion as I watched Jim's very obvious regret over the past.

Some six months after Jim's visit, preparations were made for a large dance in celebration of the German newspaper's anniversary. November 27 was the date set, a date ground into my memory as that of Jim's birth as well as Alfred's death. Everyone who had anything to do with the paper was there, as well as wives, husbands, friends, and friends of friends. Vera Lourier I remember in particular, possibly because it was her dress that I wore that night—a long, elegant evening gown, dark purple, a color I have disliked ever since. Our friend Vera was a young woman who always impressed me with her fluency in many languages, though, thinking of it now, it was natural enough that she spoke Russian since her parents spoke it, French because she grew up in France, German because she was born and lived in Germany for years, Spanish because she was living in Mexico, and English because it was the language of the American tourists who helped Vera make her living as a clothes designer and model.

On some pretext I no longer remember, I had driven alone into Mexico City the day before and was to meet with Bodo the day of the party. Of course, I spent the evening and night with Alfred. Alfred had been to a heart specialist that day, and he told me of the doctor's diagnosis, which was, in fact, an ultimatum. Alfred had to leave Mexico City—his heart was in such bad shape it could no longer sustain the extreme altitude. He was also told that hard liquor, and even coffee, would be dangerous. My immediate response was, "That's not so bad. Now you can come and live with Bodo and me in Cuernavaca. It's semitropical and almost sea-level." My pleasure at the thought of the three of us living together far outweighed any concern for

Alfred and his heart condition. His reply was a definite no—he would be unable to stand the proximity of either of us: to Bodo, because he could no longer bear the strain of the lie, loving and respecting Bodo too much; to me, because he would not be able to stand the knowledge that I preferred to remain with Bodo. He seemed, however, not to want to discuss it, possibly in order not to bother me with his troubles. We made love that night, and I remember wondering about the strain on his heart, fearing that perhaps it was too much.

The following evening at the party, I had just finished a dance with Bodo and was sitting at a small table with him and Egon Kisch when someone came over and said to us, "Please come to the bar, and try to get Alfred to stop drinking." Bodo and Egon were deep in conversation, and may not even have heard. Remembering the doctor's warning, I was horrified and ran to the bar in the next room. Alfred was standing at the bar, downing one straight whiskey after another. I went up to him, feeling something like terror, and saw his entire face dripping with sweat. He looked at me, and suddenly I didn't care that we were being watched, that no one was supposed to know that we were more than just friends. I took the handkerchief from his breast pocket and wiped the perspiration from his face while he, still looking at me, took my hand and raised it to his lips, also apparently not caring who was watching, and as he kissed my hand I heard him murmur, very softly, "Good-bye, my love." I was suddenly panic-stricken that we would be seen and heard, and I left the room. Minutes later, I was called in again, this time with definite foreboding—I was too late. I saw Alfred sprawled on the floor, clearly dead, his face and hands a ghastly yellow, and only then did his good-bye register.

In Alfred's wallet, aside from a few pesos, was a note from Jim—a note he had clearly prized deeply, for he had not shown its contents to either Bodo or me. It was a simply worded declaration of love, friendship, and respect.

Warmhearted, strong, brave, dedicated Alfred. I have often wondered why I never told him I loved him—loved his warmth, his patience with me, the firmness of his friendship and regard for Bodo, even his pain over the betrayal. I loved him, but wasn't mature enough to admit it, to tell him, or wise enough to know the years of grief I might have prevented. I could almost feel myself grow after Alfred's death, looking squarely into myself, in shame and guilt over my words and actions during the short time I had known him. I believe I felt vicariously the immensity of his unspoken despair, and I knew an almost unbearable shame over my behavior.

Some months after Alfred's death, I told Bodo about Alfred and me. I had to. I was simply unable to have sex with him; anyway, he surmised that my grieving over Alfred was deeper than that for a good friend. I told him, and added that Alfred had been in love with me. Bodo's reaction startled me. I had expected expressions of pain and fury, but instead I watched his eyes fill with tears as he moaned softly, "Oh, Alfred, you poor guy." Bodo and I stopped even trying to sleep together. We had meanwhile moved back into Mexico City, and for almost a year we lived together in friendship, even love, and awareness of our mutual caring for little Joel. Neither of us spoke again of either sex or Alfred, or of the possibility of leaving each other. It was during that year that I remember Bodo running up the two flights to our apartment to show me with pride the English translation of his novel on the Spanish Civil War, *Lieutenant Bertram*. He was pleased, not only that the book was finally published in English, but that now I would be able to read his writing in my own language.

Then Bodo fell in love. Waldeen was a young American woman—a dancer who had gained a good deal of respect as an innovator: the first to have brought modern dance to Mexico. Waldeen was not only well known as a dancer, she had also translated into English some of Pablo Neruda's best-loved poems. I remember a small volume of Pablo's translated by Waldeen that was called *Let the Railsplitter Awake*. Waldeen was leftist in her thinking, and accepted and respected by everyone around me. She had a pleasant face and a somewhat clownlike smile, the corners of her mouth tilting up into an almost perfect half circle, and she had perfect teeth. I saw her not only as my superior intellectually. She also had very large breasts, which in my naïveté I regarded as an overwhelming advantage. When Bodo told me he was in love with her, I was devastated.

The following two months were wretched ones, and it was then that I almost literally felt the loss of Jim, Alfred, and Bodo as three quick and supremely violent blows in the area of my face and chest. Unable to read, scarcely eating, I spent most of the time alone, though Bodo was still living with me. I became gradually aware that I had no friends and that, with the exception of Egon and Gisl Kisch, the other members of the group had automatically accepted Waldeen and Bodo as a couple. Alone most of the time, I occasionally even afflicted myself physically, clutching myself, digging my nails into my arms with all the strength I had, and finding some relief in the small pain I was able to cause. (Years later, during a larger loneliness and grief, I discovered the value of a yawn, during which one does not think or feel—except that a yawn cannot be prolonged, nor can it be induced.) It was then too that I came to realize the importance of work, of having something one had to do. There was nothing to distract me from myself. True, there was Joel, but I had a maid, Zita, who loved him almost as much as I did, and whose efficiency and devotion to me and to Joel left nothing for me to do. I began to think of returning to New York, and wrote Jim of my intention.

My last evening in Mexico, spent with Bodo, was strange and even wonderful. With both of us knowing I was leaving, a mysterious bond grew during the entire evening, which we spent moving from one bar and dancing place to another, drinking some, dancing, each of us keeping clear of any mention of the morning or of Waldeen, until I realized—as I know Bodo did—that we loved each other and that he did not want me to go. But neither did he ask me to stay, and I was scarcely surprised that he didn't. I wondered at first, but then remembered the story of Ellen which he told me the first night in our apartment—how, after six years together they had simply parted without a word—and I knew that, regardless of what he was feeling, he would, again, say nothing.

So Joel and I left Mexico, driving first to Laredo, where I sold the car, and taking a train the rest of the way to New York City. I did not expect ever to return to Mexico, nor did I have any expectations of New York. It did not occur to me to return to Jim—and I knew anyway that he and Mia Fritsch were now living together. But Jim did have an apartment for me and Joel—I think he just kept it, mostly empty, perhaps as a place to work or escape to, I never knew. But I was glad to have it ready for us, all furnished but unbelievably dirty. It was on Cornelia Street in Greenwich Village, a largish room with a fireplace and a small alcove with a double bed. It was hard to tell whether or not the place had been recently used, but I do remember a bathroom so neglected that I spent some four hours cleaning the toilet alone. I attacked that toilet with something like pleasure, seeing in the project a resolve to bring the shredded strings of my life together. I would get the place painted and clean first, find a day school for Joel, and then look for some means of supporting myself and Joel.

Of course, I knew there was a war going on, but I scarcely felt it, except for the time I tried to buy butter and discovered it was rationed. And I also realized there was a scarcity of workers when I tried to find someone to paint the apartment. Eventually a young man offered to help me paint at night.

Sometimes Jim took Joel, and I was glad for the respite. Joel and I were almost always together, and I knew he was lonely. I was no substitute for friends nearer his own age. He sorely missed his little Spanish-speaking friend in Mexico, Mario, and asked often for Zita and Bodo. His language was Spanish, so the English spoken all around us only increased his isolation. We went to playgrounds—I always hoping for a miracle in another child or children. There were hours spent swinging him, his small hands tight around the iron chains of the swings, his four-year-old face showing no joy. It was Christmas, and I bought toys and a small Christmas tree which we trimmed together. No one I knew had any small children to play with Joel. Once I took him to a showing of *Snow White and the Seven Dwarfs*. The witch, as ferocious as it was possible to portray her, terrified him as well as some of the other small children; mothers carried their children screaming from the movie theater. Joel bent down silently and put his head in my lap, away from the awful woman on the screen, and he didn't bring his head up until he trusted my repeated assurances that the show was over.

It was a sad and lonely stretch of time. I saw Jim, though his involvement with Mia, and my own pride—awareness of my unaccustomed state of vulnerability—caused me to keep a cool distance. I also assumed that his visits were mainly to see and come to know Joel, which was true to a great degree.

Eventually I found a good preschool for Joel, called the Little People's School. Joel had not been there long enough, fortunately, to be among those purposely exposed to the mumps after one little girl was diagnosed. The school's doctor ordered all the children to be exposed naturally, the idea being that such children's illnesses were normal and had to be gotten through. The doctor, however, had not foreseen that parents would also contract the disease, by no means without risk. Some parents became dangerously ill—and as a result of the scandal, the school was shut down.

After three lonely months in New York, I received a letter from Bodo: he too was lonely, missing Joel as well as me, and he asked us to return. His affair with Waldeen was finished, and he looked forward to a new life with Joel and me, and possibly a little brother or sister for Joel.

The letter had a predictable effect on my waning confidence—waning mainly because the thought of having to face my life without the support of a man was frightening to me. And so I set about happily making plans to return to Mexico, resolving inwardly that I would, by hook or crook, make it work with Bodo.

The night before I was to fly back to Mexico was spent with Jim—or more correctly, Joel and I spent our last night in New York at Jim and Mia's apartment. Planes left very early in the morning in those days before jets—and since Jim was driving us to the airport it was practical to spend the night at their apartment. But I scarcely remember Mia. Joel, I know, slept on the floor in a corner of the room where I spent the night—with Jim, as it turned out. And what a mysterious coincidence it was that the last time Jim and I were together should be so similar to our first coming alive to each other on a night years before in his and Olivia's apartment. Jim, once again, came to my bed during the night, and we lay together naked, neither of us feeling like making love, but whispering and crying in each other's arms, until we finally rose, woke Joel, dressed, and left for the airport.

Whatever Jim felt then, aside from expressions of love for me, I cannot know. For myself, that night was a revelation. I knew I loved him, and the bitterness was gone.

It was the last time I saw him.

In Mexico, Bodo and I went off to Lake Chapala, near Guadalajara, to begin a new life. We left Joel in Mexico City, where he was happy to be once again with Zita and Mario. True to my new resolutions, I began to type Bodo's manuscripts, like a good wife. Of course, I had no idea what I was typing, knowing no German, but I had, years before, taught myself to type and all I needed was to see the letters, in any language. I even tried with Bodo's help to do some translating into English of one of his short stories. And the long separation, together with wanting so badly for the relationship to work, even made the sex improve.

Soon after returning to Mexico City, I started playing in a string orchestra led by Sandor Roth, the violist of the Lener String Quartet, a major quartet in the thirties, whose members dispersed after the loss of their first violinist. The sound of my violin, the Jean Baptiste Villaume violin my father had bought for me many years before, together with my naturally good tone, impressed Roth enough to give me private lessons for which he asked no money. And later, when I told him I was leaving Mexico for Germany, he, knowing we needed money, bought my precious violin. For many years I was sorry I parted with that violin, and I still am. I had been almost never without it, and it had become easily my most loved possession. In fact, it represented the only object of any importance to me. Throughout my life, I have left whole households behind me, abandoning things I had thought I cared about but almost immediately forgot. Only my violin have I loved, and missed, and about it I have always wondered, Why did I sell it?

Bodo was overjoyed when I told him one day I was pregnant, and we decided to move back to Cuernavaca, where the schools and atmosphere might be better for Joel. Bodo would commute for meetings in Mexico City, and write at home. I liked the house we found, a furnished one-story L-shaped house with all its rooms leading out onto a connecting terrace at the edge of a large garden with fruit trees. It was also near the center square, or zocalo, of the town, which meant that I could get together easily with friends, sharing a table at one of the hotel terraces, shopping, or simply enjoying again Cuernavaca's semitropical climate. I sat sometimes with Dorothy, who by then was clearly an alcoholic though I still liked her, and sometimes I dropped in on Vera Lourier, who was living and working in Cuernavaca.

Nancy Johnston was the English wife of Archy Johnston, a reporter for a Mexican newspaper who later, back in England and disenchanted with English politics as well as the handling of his copy, eventually emigrated to the Soviet Union. At the time, Nancy was a horsewoman who rented out her six or seven horses, which she cared for herself, so carefully that she insisted on accompanying her clients, never allowing anyone to ride faster than a trot. I believe I was the only person she trusted with her favorite and most difficult horse, Joshua, once even leaving him in my care.

Nancy conducted a first-grade school at her home for a few lucky American children—lucky because the children, including Joel once he was six years old, were called for each morning by Nancy on Joshua, with a saddled horse for each child. After a ride through the hills around Cuernavaca the troop returned to Nancy's house, where the children unsaddled the horses and groomed and watered them. They then began their lessons on Nancy's terrace. It was ideal. The children were all happy with the arrangement, and by no means less important, Nancy was an excellent teacher.

Among Joel's friends at that time I particularly remember Chris, a beautiful blond child about six years old, who was one of the children of a retired American gangster, or so I was told and readily believed. The vast mansion where Chris lived along with assorted children of various ages, all extraordinarily beautiful, was distinguished by the two large machine guns placed at opposite corners of the grounds—to handle a possible uprising of the population, I was told. Big Bill, as the father of the children was called, rarely stayed with a woman longer than it took for her to produce a child, after which she disappeared and another lovely young woman showed up. Soon one more marvelous child would be part of Big Bill's collection. Joel and I knew only Chris, though, and I remember watching with admiration the way he sat erect and confident on a handsome, alert horse, his spotless white shorts fitting tightly around his strong, young thighs, while immediately behind him, also on an elegant horse, but in a charro outfit, came his escort, a stable boy and protector in one.

I saw Big Bill only occasionally, a large, handsome man who looked the part ascribed to him. I remember how he walked into one of the shops on the zocalo, the tails of a wildly flowered silk shirt tied across his bulging belly, the shirt unbuttoned, exposing a large, hairy chest. The store he entered was where Vera Lourier was then working, selling and modeling the lovely hand-printed, original silk-screen designs of the Canadian Tillet brothers, Jim and Leslie. The Tillets brought to Mexico a good deal of money, much talent, and ideas for original designs. They also brought good looks and good intentions, the latter including plans to help the large number of refugees from Franco Spain by giving them work in their enterprise. On the large grounds of the Tillet place were barracks for the Spanish workers. Leslie, I remember, had an immense photograph of Lenin in his office. Jim, tall and handsome, looking like a blond Tarzan, soon married Nieves, known to be Diego Rivera's first model, a beautiful young woman, half-Indian and half-Negro, Jim's counterpart in good looks. The Tillets had many parties in those days. Nieves became jealous during one of the Tillet orgies and threw a girl's fur coat into the blazing fireplace. That fireplace was extraordinary, certainly the largest in my experience. Before it stood a semicircular table with an attached semicircular bench large enough to seat roughly fifteen people. I remember Bodo and me seated on that bench, in front of each of the guests a whole freshly roasted chicken and a large bottle of white wine. That was the meal, and behind us the Tillet dogs waited for the discarded chicken bones. It was not unusual, around three in the morning, for drunken friends to find themselves in the large swimming pool, where one of the guests occasionally failed to surface and had to be dragged up by the others. I wasn't there, but I heard how they and their guests sometimes lined up on the floor on their bellies, on one side of the oversized living room, and used the Tillets' guns to shoot Coca-Cola bottles set along the far wall—or, much more reckless, tried to hit the tires of passing motorists on their way to Acapulco. John Steinbeck came to Cuernavaca around then, and went to meet the glamorous Tillets he had heard about. Jim Tillet, proud and pleased to have a visit from Steinbeck, wanted to live up to his reputation. When he finally appeared to greet the writer on the spacious terrace, he was wearing a brightly colored sarong and had a pet monkey perched atop his handsome blond head. He walked quickly toward Steinbeck, reaching out a confident hand just as the monkey let loose his bowels down poor Jim's face.

I was almost four months pregnant when Jim Agee finally sent his signature agreeing to a divorce. That bit of paper allowed me to end, for an exorbitant sum, my first marriage. Illegal as the process probably was, it nevertheless made it possible for Bodo and me to wed, which we did in Mexico City soon afterward.

It was while I was pregnant, and before the Nazis finally capitulated, that I heard of President Roosevelt's death. I don't understand why it affected me as it did, but I know it did—I remember likening the loss of Roosevelt to that of a protective father. Sharp also in my memory is the meeting, somewhere in Europe, of the American and Russian soldiers. I felt I could identify with their jubilation, seeing in it a dropping-away of not only the barriers of language, but also the differences in their separate ideologies, so that they met not just as allies with a common goal, but as brothers who could transcend the vast differences between social and political systems.

Stefan was born the first week in May, almost a year to the day after the Red army had marched into Berlin. The following months, in Cuernavaca, were joyous ones, with Joel happy in his school, and Bodo and me closer than we had ever been before. I was glad that my father came down to Mexico to see me and the new baby, and to meet Bodo. He did not believe Bodo and I were married, because he brought a ring for me—a slender gold wedding band which I placed on my bare ring finger, trying to convince him that Bodo and I were indeed man and wife. It must have been very hard for my father, conservative in his thinking, with his strong love of family and equally strong sense of paternal obligation. How often he must have wondered how I had happened at all, just as I sometimes wondered how I could have such a father, whose ideal was to mold me into a replica of a "normal American girl." He always wanted me to be dressed properly, with gloves and a hat and shoes to match, and with ideas, if I had to have them, conforming with those of the majority. But despite my very obvious tendencies in the opposite direction, he continued to love me and to help me, and over the years he stopped trying to reason with me. I continued to see in him always someone I could fall back on, who I knew would always bail me out. I was often secretly a little ashamed of his lack of education, his rigid Republicanism, and his need to impress the world with money, the only defense he had. It took many years before I learned really to love and respect my father, to know his courage and humanity, and to realize his loneliness.

With Hitler defeated, the political exiles began to make their way back to Europe. Egon and Gisl had already left for Czechoslovakia, and Bodo began making plans for our departure, which included arrangements for the four of us to be taken to Russian-occupied Germany by way of Leningrad, on a Soviet freighter. The freighter, Bodo told me, would arrive soon, at the port town of Progreso, in the Yucatán. It is difficult for me to reconstruct my thinking at that time. I know I loved the house in Cuernavaca where we had been happy, and I would naturally have preferred to remain there. Yet I was curious; I had never been to Germany. It didn't occur to me that there was anything unusual in my going or that taking two small children along might be dangerous. I know there was no faltering in my decision to accompany Bodo to a defeated and devastated country, the country responsible for the ravaging of Europe and the murder of millions. Bodo was the children's father and my husband, so feeling as I always did that somehow everything would be all right, I worked along with him on our plans to emigrate. The two boys and I needed a passport. Joel and I were both American-born, and I had registered Stefan at the American embassy, thus making him an American as well. Americans, however, were banned from travel to Germany, nor was it likely that I would receive a passport if I mentioned that our itinerary was taking us to the Soviet Union.

I cannot imagine myself doing now what I did then, which was to turn up brazenly at the American embassy in Mexico City, acting the part of a spoiled woman and demanding an immediate passport for my journey with my two children—to France. The boat was waiting, I said, and there could be no delay. The young man I spoke to assured me that he would do all he could but explained that such matters take time. After all, the passport had to come from Washington. I meanwhile did what I was told, which was to return with the proper pictures of me and the two children together. Two days later, I showed my fury that the passport was not yet available, arguing that I was in danger of missing my boat. The affable young man, visibly disturbed over my distress, said he would try to get me an emergency passport. He succeeded in that, but a few days later, a call from the embassy requested that I return with it for some technicality. Bodo advised me to ignore the request, saying they would only retract the precious document, and of course that is what they would have done, since Washington's denial of the application had obviously arrived. For all the scheming and urgency, however, it was another year and a half before Bodo and I and the two children finally left for Germany.

6 Gross-Glienicke

$\mathcal{I}$ had my passport, and with money sent by my father as well as that from the sale of my violin, we purchased supplies—sacks of rice and oatmeal, cans of Danish butter, and oil, the foods which we were told were not available in postwar Germany. The weeks went by, the money was gone, and still we have no word of the arrival of the freighter. Bodo borrowed from members of the bourgeois group, some of whom tried to dissuade me from leaving—they had heard stories of how hard life in Germany was.

One couple had left for Berlin, and two months later the wife returned, alone, to remain in Mexico. She insisted on seeing me, and recounted horror stories of the difficulties—no electricity, no heat, nothing to cook with, nothing to buy, not even bread. I listened to her, and I remember wondering why she told me such stories knowing that Bodo was leaving and that the children and I were to leave with him. Perhaps there was a part of me that wished it wasn't necessary to leave, but mainly I had absolute trust in Bodo's love and large sense of responsibility toward me and the children. I knew he wouldn't move us to Germany if he could not take care of us. Meanwhile, however, we waited, living on borrowed money and literally out of suitcases. Money had to be earned. For Bodo, a German writer, to find work in Mexico would have been virtually impossible. It was agreed that I, an American, had more of a chance. Bodo stayed in Cuernavaca with Joel and Stefan while I went to Mexico City to look for an inexpensive apartment and for a job to sustain us until the boat arrived. The Galleria Mont-Orendain, not far from where I secured an apartment, was a likely place for me to ask for work, and to my surprise I was hired immediately, to begin work the following Monday.

Bodo hired a truck—we had no money but somehow had to get our belongings into Mexico City. Thought after thought was discarded, until we eventually came up with the one person we hadn't asked for a loan. Pilar was the Spanish wife of the Czech cultural attaché in Mexico. She had visited us in Cuernavaca (her husband was usually busy), and once she had spent the day and eaten with us. I was more friendly with her than Bodo, so it seemed logical that I should be the one to approach her. Bodo was with the children in the truck on its way to Mexico City, while I got a seat in one of the tourist cars which I knew went past Pilar's house on the outskirts of the capital. When I got off the car and approached, I saw a large, pretentious mansion, and I began to have misgivings. I buried them, however. We needed the money, and even if the friendship could scarcely be called a friendship, were they not Communists? At least I was sure her husband was, and I thought all Communists were good people.

I rang the bell on the high wrought-iron gate, and waited. The *criada* who answered led me through a well-kept garden, into the house and an elegant sitting room, where she left me to announce my presence to the señora. I looked around and felt lonely. Large and beautiful as the room may have been, I was in no state to appreciate it. Besides, remembering it now, I know it was meant to impress rather than to give comfort. The lovely chairs were placed too far apart, and the overlong divan was by itself. This was a room for stiff, formal affairs, not for friendly talk. I might have felt amused at any other time, or possibly understood the need for such affluence in the home of a diplomat. But I was acutely aware of my role as petitioner, and I was accordingly intimidated. By the time Pilar came into the room, I had lost all confidence. It was morning, and she was dressed in a flowing crepe de chine dressing gown, and looked very handsome. I felt and looked drab in comparison. Her greeting, however, was bright enough: "Why, hello. What's the occasion of this visit, so early in the morning?" I told her, saying that Bodo and the two children were on their way to the city, and that we needed money to pay for the truck when it arrived, and that I would pay her back within a week. The amount I asked for was twenty-five dollars. Her smile of greeting vanished, and I thought I saw a shift to concern, but knew I was wrong when I heard her words: "I'm sorry. I can't let you have any money.

There isn't a peso in the house." I was paralyzed with shock at a refusal I hadn't expected—and I sat in my chair, frozen, feeling my eyes suddenly fill with tears, from despair perhaps, but mostly, I believe, from humiliation. Pilar looked at me for a few seconds—what went through her mind or heart I have no way of knowing, but she rose abruptly from the couch saying, "Wait a minute. I think I do have some money back in my bedroom." She disappeared, and returned with the twenty-five dollars, which I took, despising both Pilar and myself for having to thank her and reassure her that I would return it the following Thursday, which, of course, I did.

I walked the distance from Pilar's house to our new apartment, heavy with pain, and thinking of Pilar and Cuernavaca, which I didn't expect to see again.

Pilar had asked me once during a visit of hers to Cuernavaca to recommend a *criada,* which I did. The girl, Rosa, came to me some weeks later and told me that she had left the señora despite the relatively ample salary she had received. Rosa had spilled a cup of hot chocolate, which infuriated Pilar enough to scream at her as she was cleaning up the mess she had made, "You idiot! Don't ever think you're a jewel, because you're not—you were made for work!" The last I saw Rosa she was trying to make up her mind whether or not to marry a large Mexican man who clearly wanted her as a combination *criada* and bedmate and a nursemaid for his five children.

And I remembered Maria, who couldn't have been more than thirteen when she turned up at our door asking for work. She brought with her only the torn dress on her back, saying she had run away from home. I never knew where she came from. She could have told me anything, but I was intrigued with her: she was unusually pretty, and lighter skinned than most Indian girls. Maria had cut off her long braids before I knew her. She told me it made her look less like an Indian. She stayed in the one-room shack behind our house—*criadas* never lived in the apartment or house with the family. The clothes I gave her included a pair of pajamas, which I told her were to be put on at night, to sleep in. She giggled at the idea—she had never heard of anyone wearing something different to sleep in. But she loved her pajamas, and wore them constantly, day and night, until one morning she did not come back from a short errand in town. Hours went by, and Bodo and I began to worry. The light was still on in her room, and all her precious belongings, the things I had given her, were still there. I went to the zocalo to look for her, and finally someone told me that a girl—"Yes, she had short hair"—had been seen going off with two women and a man she had been talking with. I went home, feeling with a heavy heart that I was not going to see Maria again, but I left the light on in her room for almost a week, waiting and hoping. It would have been useless to go to the police—they would simply have laughed at me.

I liked working at the gallery. It was new, a handsome duplex with a plate-glass front facing the Calle de Londres. Two young men ran it: Daniel Mont and Gabriel Orendain. Daniel was a bright, round-faced, thickly set young Mexican whose family had provided the money for the venture, one of a series of projects the Mont family had hoped would finally launch their adored Daniel on a successful career. I liked Señor and Señora Mont when I met them later. They seemed simple and unpretentious among their well-to-do surroundings, and their single-minded hope for Daniel was disarming. Daniel did, eventually, make a financial "killing," through a real-estate venture staked by his family. I was already in Europe when I heard that he had become a millionaire almost overnight. Then, only a few months later, he died suddenly of a heart attack. He must have been in his thirties. Gabriel, also very young, was a tall, elegant, fair-skinned Spaniard whose aristocratic family had lived in Mexico for generations. Despite his somewhat haughty appearance, he was friendly and extremely likable—an unabashed homosexual who, though not at all "swishy," would stoop with both knees close together and to the side when retrieving something from the floor.

Neither Daniel nor Gabriel was a businessman, nor did either of them, as far as I could see, know much about painting. They hired me—who knew even less—as a combination receptionist, organizer, bookkeeper, and salesperson. Of course I had no experience. Gabriel told me much later that he had been intrigued by my green eyes, but I suspect that my being an American with some knowledge of Spanish helped. At any rate, I soon learned how little everyone else knew about painting, except the artists themselves. Even the collectors, the connoisseurs, seemed unaware of my ignorance, for I had to bluff, and bluff I did, brazenly. A small, thickly painted Rufino Tamayo gouache, called *The Dentist*, seemed like an oil to me, and I sold it as such, for much more than it was worth, to a wealthy collector. Many years later, in Mexico, I met Mr. Lindau, the buyer, and he thanked me profusely—deadpan—for making him the owner of one of Tamayo's finest paintings. It is now, naturally, worth many times what he paid for it.

Diego Rivera, as well as David Alfaro Siqueiros, had their smaller paintings placed in most of the major galleries of Mexico City, including the Mont-

Orendain. But José Clemente Orozco, for reasons difficult to fathom, trusted no gallery except ours, and we had many of his smaller easel paintings on consignment. I say his reasons were difficult to fathom, because Daniel and Gabriel behaved no differently from most other owners of galleries, which was to lie, whenever possible, about the amount of money paid for a work and to calculate the artist's percentage on the lower fictitious amount. But Orozco trusted us. Perhaps he was attracted to the extremely affable and unorthodox manners of the owners, and their obvious lack of business sense. The gallery was also an unusually good place to show pictures. The walls were of a very light, narrowly paneled wood, and the gallery itself was always bright and inviting. Gabriel, with unerring taste, had placed lush flowering plants around spare pieces of handsome light furniture, and a winding metal staircase led to a smaller second floor and balcony with more paintings and, far back, a kind of carryall space storing discarded furniture, rolls of material, and some art work. The general atmosphere was more than pleasing—one felt immediately at home, and owing to the discreetly placed seats, plants, and low tables with ashtrays, no one who entered felt compelled to restrict attention to the pictures, far less to buy one. Perhaps that was why the gallery kept floundering.

From behind my kidney-shaped desk, made of the same blond wood as the walls, I greeted visitors, friends, potential buyers, and occasionally curious passersby. And then there were the artists, some of whom turned up almost every day: Federico Cueco, always with a small copper disk on which he was engraving. Xavier Guerrero, a heavyset, dark-skinned Indian, of whom I was particularly fond, and whose work was considered in a class with the big three of Mexican revolutionary artists. Leopoldo Mendez, an active Communist, as were many of the others, and a member of the Taller Gráfico de Arte Popular, a group of talented left-wing graphic artists. Mendez' woodcuts of the 1910 Mexican Revolution are now famous, and priced accordingly. Alfaro Siqueiros, a friend of Bodo's, almost never came to the gallery, though I remember some of his smaller pictures there. Diego Rivera dropped in occasionally, possibly to check on sales. He also used the gallery each Tuesday evening to give art lectures to American tourists. The lectures, though usually instructive, were always witty, often lewd, and invariably insulting to the audience. The tourists loved them, and chuckled at his pointed witticisms, seemingly unaware that the target was themselves. It was during one of those evenings that I listened to Diego give, as his own, a description of the United

States as the only country which had passed from barbarism to decadence without having touched civilization. Orozco came less often. I remember him at only one reception, when Gabriel asked me to sit near him and pay him as much attention as possible: "He likes pretty women." I suppose that meant I didn't need to be anything else.

Orozco, with his heavy Indian face and thick glasses, seemed remote and not easy to know, but I liked him. Once Gabriel and Daniel bought, for a few hundred pesos, a small black chalk drawing with Orozco's signature. Orozco was upstairs, near the winding staircase, when both Gabriel and Daniel showed him the drawing. After a quick glance, he turned apoplectic, and I watched him snatch the picture from Daniel, tear it up, and throw the pieces to the floor, shouting, as he stamped on them with both feet, "That's not mine!"

He was an intense nationalist. "My pictures belong in Mexico," he told me once. That was at the Orozco home, where I was trying to negotiate a sale for a friend of the gallery. Orozco, knowing the potential buyer was from the United States, had set his price so high as to make a purchase unlikely, and the picture was never sold. For Mexicans, his prices were relatively reasonable. His wife, on the other hand, was an astute businesswoman who knew very well the value of her husband's work, and was often not in agreement with the lower prices he was wont to ask of his own people.

I liked the fierceness of Orozco's integrity. He seemed so much the pure, single-minded revolutionary. And his behavior was as definitive, in this respect, as were his paintings. Yet he had charm, the very special charm of the ugly man who likes, and is liked by, women—except that one wonders, remembering the series of small easel paintings, all of women, which hung in our gallery. These were painted with the heavy, bold, even violent strokes typical of Orozco, and they showed an undeniable hatred of his subjects. There were six of them, none were sold, at least during my time at the gallery, nor can I imagine anyone's wanting them hanging on the walls.

Orozco's great revolutionary murals, like Rivera's and Siqueiros', "decorate" official buildings all over Mexico—a steady reminder of the Mexican government's interest in art as well as of the contradictions for which Mexico is famous. For in what other country can one see, displayed at a hall of justice, a mural depicting Justice itself in chains? It is one of Orozco's finest murals.

Diego Rivera, heavy-lidded and thick-lipped, also had charm and, like all the great Mexican muralists, was a full-blooded Indian. I guess *colorful* best describes Diego's personality. He liked notoriety and seemed to enjoy getting into scrapes, even using, on occasion, the gun he always carried, though I never heard of any serious harm done to anyone. One of the greats, as he certainly was, he did not seem to have the sober integrity of either Orozco or Siqueiros, and did stoop sometimes to painting, in the unmistakable Rivera style, a pretty Indian girl complete with braids and sombrero—it was the kind of picture many North Americans liked and for which they paid well.

I used to look forward to the receptions and special shows that we gave, sending out invitations to the press, collectors, artists, and friends. For me, those evenings were mainly gala affairs, and I know that Gabriel and Daniel saw them too, aside from perhaps a sale or new contact, as an excuse for a party. During the reception itself, everyone was formally dressed, and elaborate hors d'oeuvres, with cocktails or whiskey, were served by a white-coated butler. But after the last "proper" guest had left, Gabriel and Daniel pulled down the heavy metal blinds to shut out the street, and the real partying began. I was invariably invited to stay, but never did, knowing that Bodo and the two children were at home waiting for me.

One of the daytime visitors to the gallery was a Señor Rafael, a wealthy Mexican who possessed the largest collection of Orozco's easel paintings anywhere. Señor Rafael became interested in a small Orozco at the gallery, and Gabriel, after a long afternoon of cocktail drinking and discussion with the client, finally succeeded in making the sale—an important one because the gallery was in trouble and there were bills to be paid. Señor Rafael gave Gabriel his personal check for a large amount of some thousands of pesos. When I was ready to leave for home, Gabriel stopped me, asking that I deposit the check as soon as the bank opened the following morning. I was thirty-four years old then, but I remember very well the pride I felt in being entrusted with the responsibility and the sense I had of being suddenly grown-up. The following morning, I displayed the check to Bodo, who was lying in his bath. I have always secretly believed that something unnatural did it, because I was not near the tub, for suddenly the check fluttered out of my hand and into the bath water. Quick as we both were, it was too late—the signature was almost illegible. At the bank, the teller naturally refused it, and my explanations and pleas with the bank manager did no good either. I walked fast, sometimes running, the many blocks to the main branch and the bank manager there. Yes, he knew Señor Rafael and was acquainted with his signature, but no, sorry, impossible, "We must have a new check." And so I finally had to face the humiliation of getting another check; by then it was after ten o'clock. A taxi took me to the address of Señor Rafael, a large mansion suiting a Mexican with money and taste. And I was led, by the servant who admitted me, through room after elegant room until I was eventually shown into a bright, sunlit sitting room and the presence of Señor Rafael. Señor Rafael, however, was not alone. Standing by a latticed window was Gabriel, who for whatever reason was visiting just then. So, never good at lying, I explained the entire matter, bathtub and all. I need not have suffered so much, however—Señor Rafael walked immediately to a small desk and wrote another check, while Gabriel, decent as he was, showed nothing of the amusement he must have felt.

I was still working at the gallery when I heard about a scandal concerning Diego Rivera's large and very beautiful mural in the Hotel del Prado. Diego had painted the words "Dios no existe" ("There is no God") on a satchel which one of the figures in the mural was holding. When the picture was unveiled on a large interior wall of the hotel, there was, of course, wonder and excitement at first—it was one of Rivera's best murals—but then, on closer examination, the words were discovered, and in the uproar the mood changed from appreciation to indignation, resulting in someone's furiously scratching out the words. I was sitting at my desk at the gallery when I heard from some of the artists that they were going to accompany Diego, who just as indignant and also with a good deal of self-righteousness, had heard of the censorship and was on his way to the hotel. I was alone and couldn't leave the gallery, or I would have had the pleasure of being among the group of supporters who went with Diego. At the hotel, he took the ready brush that someone handed him and painted his words back in place, where they still are.

During my almost two years of working at the gallery, Bodo was at home taking care of the children, seeing to the maid, the meals, the apartment, and of course, his own work and meetings. I accepted his role then without much thought; after all, I was earning the money. But I now realize how remarkable he was—not that it wasn't a fair exchange, but Bodo accepted quietly and responsibly, even with dignity, a role which, in those years, normally belonged to women. We each of us fell easily into our place, nor do I remember any quarrels or strife between us. Despite the strong friendship, interdependence, even love between us, sex continued to be a problem, however, and neither of us seemed able to face squarely the glaring fact that we simply did not get along in bed—something we neither discussed nor considered in planning our move to Germany.

At last, the Soviet freighter which was to take us to Leningrad arrived at

Progreso, and after I left my job at the gallery, the four of us flew in a small Mexican plane to that seaport town. We spent a memorable night there, at what the taxi driver assured us was the "best hotel in town." As it turned out, it was the only hotel, a dilapidated one-story building which, to my dismay, turned out to be more a whorehouse than a hotel. The enormous room we were led to had two large double beds, each covered with filthy, even blood-stained sheets. The mosquito netting had large, gaping holes—it was July and could not have been hotter or muggier any place in the world. I particularly remember the large bathroom with its floor covered with dirty water and a half toilet that had better be left undescribed. I worried for the children: would they survive a night in Progreso without getting sick? Malaria was my main fear. I spent the night outside the room, near the entrance to the establishment, holding Stefan in my arms and watching the couples enter, coo at my two-year-old infant, and leave a half hour later. I don't know where or how Joel and Bodo spent the night.

It was lovely, though, early the following morning. I was alone with the two children on the beach, waiting for Bodo to finish what remained to be done prior to our boarding. Far off, we could see the outline of the boat, which, to me, was waiting only for us. The beach was a marvel after the horrors of the previous night. There was even a slight breeze. The air and sand felt clean, and my worries over malaria seemed remote.

I still have the large conch shell I found that morning, and I can still see it as I first saw it—perched high on the sand, the only object on that long stretch of clean, lovely sand.

Anyone who has ever crossed the ocean by boat knows what a very special experience it is—the living from day to day, involved in matters and people related to the boat, without much thought of what one has left behind, or what is expected on the other side. That stretch of time, whether it is one or five weeks, is for its duration all there is—a kind of life within a life, perhaps something like a pregnancy when thoughts are limited to the nine months of growth, with a minimum of thought or responsibility beyond that time, or a kind of Zen living, involved only in the *now* of that stretch of time on the sea. At least so it has been for me on the four occasions when I have made sea crossings between Europe and America, feeling on each of them that luxurious suspension of time.

Our trip on a Soviet freighter called the *Dmitri Donskoy* took just five weeks, during which that life within a life was lived to its fullest. I thought only once of arriving in Leningrad, the day I thought I had forgotten to pack a lipstick. When I asked the first mate, Ivan, with whom I had become friendly, if a lipstick would be available in Russia, he answered with one of the few English words he knew—words that frequently expressed the opposite of what he meant. His grinning, confident affirmation using the word *impossible* had me confused for a while.

We shared our cabin with one other passenger, a German woman named Gerda, also on the way to Germany by way of Leningrad. The cabin was small, with scarcely enough bunk space for all of us, and Gerda's daily habits were often annoying when they weren't downright funny. She had a compulsion to wash her hands almost continuously and almost nonstop; she was in her midthirties, with a fear of drooping facial muscles, so that when she wasn't washing her hands, one could hear her patting her face, speedy little pats using a quick upward motion of the hands, which she said was guaranteed to ward off age. Gerda was also afraid of becoming ill on the Russian food. We all ate together at the same long table with the captain and sailors and the only other passengers on board, a Russian family returning from its stay at the Mexican embassy. The same food was served each day: borscht—but it was delicious—with great hunks of cabbage and pork, served with large pieces of Russian rye bread. Gerda, however, was afraid of it, and tried to explain her delicate stomach to the cook, and her need for white toast, the quest for which she gave up when she received the results of the cook's efforts to please her; I think he put some white bread in a closed damp box, allowing it to age for a few days before use. So our friend never sat at the table with us, and when she wasn't patting her face or washing her hands, she was in a corner of the cabin nibbling noisily on saltines. The last I saw of her was in the luxurious dining room of the Intourist hotel in Leningrad, where she had ordered and was happily eating the rich, sumptuous, and sophisticated food available there.

The sailors were a jolly lot. They worked hard, they were always friendly, and I enjoyed watching them occasionally grab large onions from an enormous pile they passed on deck. They bit into them, munching them like apples. The sailors were overjoyed at having my two small children on board and set about almost immediately to construct a veritable playground, including an extremely well made swing which we took to Germany with us.

Excitement mounted among the sailors as we approached Leningrad, and a few hours before our arrival, their exhilaration reached such a pitch that they all began to dance together. It was fun to watch them, and I remember how I, infected with their gaiety, ran with my friend the first mate to the hold to fetch some Louis Armstrong records.

Leningrad, one could see, was still a lovely city despite the German bombing in some areas. It was not long after the blockade that had lasted a year and a half, and everyone in the streets looked pinched. We were told that most surviving Leningraders suffered from heart trouble, and of course, there were no animals. Even the mice had been eaten.

We stayed at the Intourist hotel, not far from the big Nevsky Prospect street. We were, it seemed, guests of the government, a result of Bodo's activities as an active antifascist and Communist. The hotel had retained its elegance from before the Revolution, and my memory now sees an impressive Greek Orthodox priest, in full regalia, with a long, full white beard, slowly walking down the wide gilt stairway. I didn't know where he was going or where he came from, but his presence seemed particularly incongruous alongside the group of five stern German women, clearly invited guests and comrades, in sensible suits and shoes, who were climbing up and down the same stairs. Bodo spent much of the time arranging for our passage to Germany, and I could not move around much with the two children. We did do some sightseeing, however; we visited the Hermitage and spent a lot of time with a young Russian girl who spoke some English.

I don't recall how I met Wanda, and I don't know how representative she was of the Russian people then. But it was shocking to realize how deep was her dislike of Jews, though to her knowledge she had never personally known any. They were the cause of all misery; the hotel where we were staying, she said, housed Jews, and she was convinced she could tell a Jew from ordinary people. When I told her finally that I was Jewish, she was dismayed and confused, and I suspect she did not quite believe me. Her anti-Semitism, together with her frank and open admiration of Germans, was particularly strange in view of what had happened to her some years previously. Wanda, eighteen years old at the time we met her, was living with her mother, an engineer. A visit to her lodging one afternoon showed what I learned was the usual apartment-sharing situation in Russian cities: a communal bathroom and kitchen, and strangers wandering to and fro in her one room—which apparently did not seem strange to Wanda. Her father had been killed in the war, after which she lived with her grandmother in a small town occupied by the Germans while her mother went to work in Berlin. "Every day," she said in her broken

English, "I saw people hanging in the village square. I was scared, so I stayed mostly at home." Her grandmother worked, she said, and one day she failed to come home. "It got later and later, and I was so scared I cried." She must have been crying very loud—perhaps screaming in fear—because two Nazi soldiers eventually came into the courtyard. "They each had a gun and I saw the Nazi sign on their arms and their caps. I stopped crying and just looked at them, and they were talking together in German. I thought that they were going to kill me, because one of them pointed his gun at me, but the other then said something, pointing to my hair and eyes." Wanda had blue eyes and blond hair, and if the two Nazi soldiers didn't shoot her for disturbing them with her crying, it was obviously because of her coloring—in their terms, Aryan features to be protected. Wanda lived through that ordeal—her grandmother finally returned—but she continued to admire Germans and despise Jews.

That September of 1948 was cold and rainy in Germany, especially on the Baltic Sea, at Ahrenshoop, where the two children and I stayed for a few weeks while Bodo was in Berlin to find living quarters for us.

I spoke no German, nor did either of the children. We lived in a room near the shore, and about a mile and a half from a place where we could get meals. Three times a day, often in the rain and always in the cold, I carried the two-year-old, Stefan, with the eight-year-old, Joel, walking by my side, to and from the Kurhaus, our eating place. I do not remember particularly minding the meager food that was offered, concerned as I was mainly that the children be adequately fed. For the rest, I had prepared myself for such miserable conditions in postwar Germany that none of it seemed especially bad. Nor did I fear for the months ahead, remembering the supplies we had brought: oil, bags of rice, soap, and canned butter—precious items most Germans did not have.

The meals in Ahrenshoop were mainly great mounds of boiled potatoes and occasionally some mushrooms. At breakfast, bread, an imitation coffee with a name that sounded very strange to my ears: Muckefuck. There also was a kind of jam, made without either fruit or sugar, which tasted a little like soap. Once, though, we were served some pieces of apple tart, which I decided we should carry home for later. Rain is never warm in Germany, even in summer, and that September evening the rain was penetratingly cold as we trudged along, trying to avoid the puddles in the dirt road. Then Joel suddenly slipped, stumbled, and dropped the precious bits of apple tart. I swung at him in a frenzy of anger and frustration, and slapped him hard. I instantly, and ever since, have regretted that.

I remember little else of those dreary weeks in Ahrenshoop, aside from the ice-cold water with which I tried to bathe the children as quickly as possible. Trying to dry off one of the boys, I broke a little porcelain soap dish. I was horrified, knowing the impossibility of buying or replacing *anything*.

I felt little sympathy for the people around me. It is hard to feel compassion in the face of such abject self-pity. Besides, I had just arrived from Leningrad, and here were the Germans, whose soldiers had invaded the Soviet Union and blockaded Leningrad, complaining about their lot—yet they all seemed in so much better shape than the Russians did. I saw no one without shoes, for instance, either in Ahrenshoop or later in Berlin; in fact, some wore very good shoes, while many Russians had to do without, despite the coming cold. German faces on the whole were pinched and bitter, as were the Russian faces, but I was to hear from too many Germans—some spoke a little English—an often-repeated tale of woe in which there invariably figured expressions of humiliation at having lost to the Russians, or of pity for themselves. The recurring theme was "We Germans don't deserve this—we are better than the primitive Russians."

I was glad when Bodo finally came and we went on to Berlin, and eventually to the house Bodo had procured for us, in Gross-Glienicke, some twenty miles from Berlin's center. I still remember my shock and disbelief at my first sight of Berlin—prepared as I thought I was for a city in ruins. Even though there were sections of the city seemingly untouched, it was hard to imagine anything worse than what I witnessed. Skeletons of buildings showing the interior walls with shreds of flowered wallpaper still visible, occasionally a door leading nowhere, and everywhere piles of rubble, mortar yet to be removed. Groups of women, called *Trümmerfrauen,* literally "rubble women," worked as volunteers clearing the debris in their home areas. They had a special look, these *Trümmerfrauen:* somewhat bedraggled and with their hair hidden beneath large kerchiefs tied on top, turban style, to protect them from the dirt and dust. The few faces of Berliners I saw in the streets were grim-looking, and one wondered where they were going—certainly not shopping, since there was nothing to buy in what was left of most businesses. I do remember one shop's display of lampshades—but who would want one? There were no light bulbs, nor was there much electricity, and I became used to candlelight during the dark winter afternoons and evenings.

Almost immediately on beginning our new lives in Gross-Glienicke, I became aware of the constant booming of the planes directly over our house. It was the airlift, bringing food and supplies to Berlin, in response to the Russians' blockade of the road and waterways serving the western-controlled parts of the city. It was impossible to escape the political tension between our area and the three western sectors of Berlin; it was always there, even though day-to-day practical living had to go on. The talk was inevitably political, with the sectors and borders scarcely a half mile away, and the airlift constantly roaring overhead.

The realization came somewhat abruptly that Bodo's and my roles had radically changed. In Mexico, I had been independent—I spoke Spanish, even worked and earned money. In Germany, without knowing the language and aware of the traumatic situation of most of the people, I felt—and was almost numb with—helplessness. And Bodo, as patient and responsible as ever, handled everything, from grocery buying and hiring a woman to help with the housework, to arranging for a German tutor for Joel. It was a pattern that continued even after I learned sufficient German to get along, so that my memory of the twelve years I lived in Germany is one of chronic dependence.

Frau Lohman, our housekeeper, was a youngish woman whose husband, a German soldier, had not returned from the front. Frau Lohman knew enough of Bodo's role in the changed Germany to keep her thoughts to herself, but when she gazed dreamily into a distant field or spoke of the lovely things her husband had brought back from Denmark or Bulgaria, I also knew enough not to speak of how he had secured those beautiful leather boots or silk underwear and blouses. When she came each day from her own house in the western (English-occupied) sector, she arrived with her rations, real butter and even ham, which always seemed to be superior to the rations in the eastern (Russian) zone. But we didn't live badly: apart from the supplies we had brought with us, Bodo, as an active antifascist fighter and writer, received additional and superior allotments, in food as well as living quarters, and each month there was a package of extra sausage, bread, and cooking oil. The house we were given had not been long vacated. There were still a few hundred pounds of potatoes in the basement—potatoes which had not yet sprouted—and also dozens of delicate glass phials of varying sizes. These intrigued me until I learned that one of the sons of the previous owner had been an amateur chemist. The family—the mother was Jewish, her husband "Aryan"—had been forced to sell the house for a pittance to some local Nazi, and had emigrated to England.

We lived in that house for seven years. It was well built and expensive, and seemed to reflect the elegant taste of the previous owners, who had clearly been well-off. I was especially intrigued with the bathroom, with the large ashtray enclosed in the wall next to the toilet, and the intercom bell one could ring if one needed help while bathing or showering. The house was not uncommonly big—three bedrooms upstairs—yet there was an intercom system in the kitchen through which one could speak or receive messages from any of the other rooms, a gadget obviously meant for communicating orders to a servant. The house seemed perfect, with its large living room and fireplace, and terraces, one of which led down to the lake, for swimming in the summer, and ice-skating in the winter.

Bodo saw to all practical matters. I soon realized that in Russian-occupied territory and in his own country and among his own people he was an important person with important responsibilities. Impressed at first, I soon began to take for granted the reflected glory of being his wife. Because Bodo was not only a widely read writer but also chief editor of the magazine *Aufbau* (Construction), the main literary publication of the East, he became secretary of the PEN Club and he was a member of the Academy of Arts and an official of the Writers' Union. I came to realize too that Bodo's activities and status allowed him not only the house we lived in, but also a car and driver, provided and paid for by the publishing house. The driver, Jochen, was a lively young blond mechanic, affable, efficient, and obviously intrigued with me as an American. We all became dependent on him. He not only drove Bodo back and forth to work, but was relied on for everything from babysitting and grocery shopping to mechanical chores around the house and even the selection of servants. There was nothing exploitative in any of it, not only because Jochen was well paid for his time, but also because there was a genuine liking among us. It is difficult to imagine those years without him, those years while the language and people were still a riddle to me. There was no riddle to penetrate concerning Bodo's friends, who soon became my own—writers like Bodo, artists, professionals, or simply intelligent people who were as avidly anti-Nazi as we were. It was different with the general populace, Germans who had remained in Germany during the war. I rarely trusted them, and even later, when I could speak a little German, I seldom believed their fervent denials of any knowledge of Nazi evils. One woman, however, was openly against the Nazis. Her sister had been in a concentration camp for dating a Pole, and she told me of an event which no one else in the entire village had apparently seen. A long straggling line of old men and young boys had been driven at a run through the town by Nazi officers on horseback. There were cries and pleas in vain for water, she said, and it was in full view of the town residents.

We also had a succession of maids, mostly from the countryside, who had been thoroughly infected with Nazism. The maid whom I cared for most, and who continued to be my friend even after we moved to Berlin, came to us as a full-fledged young Nazi who, when she was ten years old, had slept with Hitler's picture under her pillow. Lilo's previous place of employment had been with a woman whose two sons had been killed in the war and who stated, our maid assured us, that had she been blessed with a third son, she would gladly have sacrificed him for Hitler. One of Lilo's duties had been to take out the sons' uniforms twice a year to clean and press them. Lilo stayed with us a long time, and eventually married a young steelworker who had become a Communist. I remember now another maid, also from the country, who had apparently been reared in the old feudal manner to look up to whoever was in charge, as to some kind of deity. I remember her as being slovenly—I had always thought Germans were so clean and orderly—but her main characteristic, which was unchangeable and continued to puzzle me, was her manner of never looking at or addressing me directly. So she would gaze off into the distance while asking, "Does Frau Uhse want me to change the sheets today?"

The People's Republic of China came into being, and Bodo, about a year after we arrived, was invited to travel there. So for three months I was alone with the two children, but not lonely; there was Jochen to look after practical matters, which he did at least as well as Bodo, and by that time I had friends in Gross-Glienicke, among them Betina and Heini Bertsch.

Heini was not a Communist but, as a chemist and important professional, was well paid by the government and chose to remain in the East. Betina was the most nearly perfect and the best-organized housekeeper I was ever to know. Their large and luxurious house, also on the lake, was always clean and orderly despite two small children—there was no maid, and Betina regularly baked, and canned vegetables and fruit grown in their large garden. She even canned eggs, and many weeks before Christmas, she was preparing and baking cookies, barrels full, one whole room of them, to send to relatives. I remember comparing myself to the grasshopper who frolicked all summer while the industrious ant prepared for the winter, though I don't remember the winters as particularly barren. The Bertsch children were extraordinarily well behaved, and in accordance with the correct bourgeois German style, the little boy always bowed and sometimes clicked his heels, and his sister curtsied, when being introduced. Neither child entered the living room, which was for adults only—the exception being the good-night ritual, when the children entered the immaculate room to show their respect to guests and to give their father and mother a good-night kiss. Heini always sat at the table in his special dining chair, and ate with his wife only when guests were present. Otherwise, he was served by Betina—special goodies, fine cheeses and sausages, which he had purchased in West Berlin, because he was a sensualist and loved good food. And Betina herself dined with the children, on simpler fare. She occasionally did have a servant in for special cleaning, and her orders were cool, crisp, and not to be misunderstood. The servant seemed to appreciate the distance between them.

The Bertsches, both Betina and Heini, spoke English and, despite the enormous differences between us, liked me and, very possibly, were intrigued by what they believed were my American ways. Knowing no other Americans, they likely thought all Americans were as unorganized and irregular as I, and as lax and permissive with children.

In the house next to the Bertsches lived Herbert and Usch Gessner; she was to become my close friend during the years I remained in Germany. Herbert had come from West Germany. He hated the Nazis and Hitler with a fury that drove him to the East to work with the Communists. Herbert, a first-rate radio commentator—whom I remember mainly as a volatile and attractive man who drank and chain-smoked—loved racing cars, was in love with his wife, and then, inexplicably, committed suicide, leaving Usch to complete alone a life which had been tragic even before she had married Herbert. Usch, also from West Germany, was half-Jewish—and when her father, a doctor and head of a large hospital in Cologne, was asked by the Nazis to divorce his Jewish wife, he refused. So Usch's mother was not carried away, but he was removed from his post at the hospital and forced to do manual labor, and Usch remembered a wretched childhood, including having to work as a maid in the homes of Aryan families. After the war she joined Herbert Gessner in becoming a Communist and avid anti-Nazi in the East.

Some time after Bodo's return from China, I became pregnant, and the next few months were spent in an agonizing effort to find a doctor who would perform an abortion. It was too late, Bodo said, to begin again; he was not quite forty-eight years old. But I wanted the baby, although I was not vocal about it. The abortion was eventually accomplished when I was in the fifth month, through the help of Jochen, who drove me to a doctor in West Berlin. The process was possibly the most disagreeable as well as the most painful experience I was ever to endure, both physically and psychologically. There followed a monthlong depression, and Bodo, clearly suffering guilt, was quietly solicitous, even to the degree of bringing coffee and orange juice to me every morning, until he finally hit on the right antidote for my depression: a horse. With Roland, three years old and recently gelded, my life took a fresh turn. Jochen helped to construct a manger in the back part of an oversized garage, and we even built a small corral. And while Joel and Stefan were in school, I happily groomed Roland, and cleaned the stable, and in the mornings before the others were awake, I was with my horse, feeding him, listening to the quiet, pleasant sound of his munching, just looking at him, and of course, riding him.

The house next door to ours was much bigger, and we had a succession of neighbors, including Friedl and Alfred (Kantor) Kantorowitz, a writer and journalist who later became embittered by the Ulbricht regime and defected to West Berlin. A large German family, the Beimers, also lived there for a while—seven beautifully behaved children, each of whom had his or her allotted chores and who never seemed to quarrel or look disheveled, children who, like the Bertsch children, filled me with wonder and unease. I remember nothing about their parents except that the father had worked as a Nazi doctor in occupied Poland, and that both father and mother were, when we knew them, strong Communists. The turnabout may or may not have been sincere, but Bodo and I never trusted the Beimers enough to extend our contact beyond polite hellos across the fence.

When the Beimer family left, the house was occupied by a large number of Russian soldiers, at least twenty of them. Occasionally we saw an officer. They were a noisy, jolly bunch and seemed to have so much fun together it was infectious. They danced on the wooden deck near the water until all hours of the night, and I can still hear in my mind's ear the sound of the Russian music—one of them played an accordion—and their singing, stamping, and laughter. Sometimes I tried to communicate with them, an effort which only convinced me of the importance of a shared language, without which two people can find themselves merely staring at each other in complete impotence. But I knew they were mostly lonely in Germany—far away from their villages in some remote part of Russia.

One of them once indicated a wish to ride Roland, and to the delight of his companions he almost got thrown as he galloped up and down the field across the street, waving a long stick cossack fashion. When another soldier one day, obviously homesick, haltingly offered in sign language to help our maid hang the wash on the clothesline, the girl panicked, convinced he was going to rape her. Eventually she relaxed and allowed him to help, and I watched his homely peasant face slowly change into a slow smile as his loneliness dissipated. Fraternizing was not permitted between Germans and Russians, and the rule was, on the whole, closely observed. I felt sorry for the Russian soldiers, though, so many hundreds of miles from home and in a country and among people who despised them. Once, in a small grocery store, I witnessed a Russian officer trying to purchase something and not being able to make himself understood. The four or five Germans in the store not only refused to help him, likely aware of what he was trying to communicate, but they were silent and openly contemptuous. Not knowing enough German myself, or how else to express my sympathy, I smiled at him in as friendly a way as I could. My good intentions were misunderstood, however, as the officer started an elaborate flirtation as soon as I left the store.

My only other encounter with the Russians came about one late afternoon when I went off through the woods on Roland. I had about an hour before the children and Bodo would be home for supper. I went at a brisk trot, scarcely aware of or caring about the direction, on and on past a sign in Russian which I did not understand, and then, suddenly, still trotting on, I heard a loud call or rather command: *Stoi!* I heard it at about the moment that I had decided to turn around anyway, and after I did, the command came again, this time unmistakably, an almost hysterical order. And as Roland and I returned to our original direction, I saw, standing, feet apart in the middle of the path, two young soldiers, each with a machine gun pointing at me. They looked frightened. I knew instinctively that if I didn't stop immediately, they would almost surely shoot. As I reined in, one of them grabbed the horse and there was an unmistakable command to dismount. I knew no Russian, of course. They conversed excitedly for a moment; then one of them, still holding the horse by the bridle, took my arm, while the other disappeared at a run. Soon there were three more Russian soldiers, all talking together excitedly, and there was clearly a question of what to do with me. I had no papers on me, and the only two words I knew and hoped would help were *Amerikansky* and *Komunist*. Neither, though, seemed to have an effect. I was finally walked, along with Roland, to a large truck, the kind with two facing bench-like affairs in back, and I had to climb up and onto the truck, where I sat opposite one of the soldiers, and we drove off—to the main barracks in Potsdam, as I learned later. Roland followed us at a gallop, ridden by another soldier, who managed to remain aloft despite the long dangling stirrups. At Potsdam, I was taken into a room with a dozen Russian officers, for questioning. Of course, I immediately made a motion showing a wish to use a telephone. The telephone, however, was not working. So I sat on a chair facing a desk, while the officers milled about me in the small room, talking in their own tongue, intermittently glancing at me. I had no idea what was going on. One officer, I remember, looked me up and down, pointedly, and I was vaguely frightened, while another's gestures told me he was convinced, and was trying to convince the others, that I was a clever spy and fully conversant in Russian. I realized that they were waiting for someone to come who could speak German; meanwhile I was offered candy from a dish on the desk, and a glass of water. When a German-speaking officer finally showed up, I was taken to another room to be interrogated—I believe it was a mess hall, because he sat across from me on a long bench and between us was a long wooden table. His German wasn't nearly as good as my own had become, and I remember his habit of striking the table pointedly and frequently with a riding crop. He obviously didn't know whether to believe my story of being an innocent American wife of a Communist living in the Russian sector. I realized by then that I had ridden past a sign in Russian warning me to go no farther; apparently, an ammunition dump was located ahead. It was only after more than three hours of interrogation that the idea came to me. I asked with sign language for a pencil and paper—and it was my final effort to explain myself.

I handed my drawing to the officer, who showed it to his companions, and they crowded around the little piece of paper. I heard, over and over again, the words *Dmitri Donskoi* spoken with wonder as they kept looking my way.

It seemed to work, but at that moment there was a commotion and Bodo entered with Jochen.

By car they had followed Roland's tracks through the woods and toward the ammunition dump, purposely getting arrested in the knowledge that they would find me quicker that way. They were right, of course, and after I was freed, I was taken to Roland, who had been tied to a fence all those hours and was almost impossible to mount, let alone ride behind the car carrying Bodo and Jochen. Not only was he in a frenzy to get home to his feed, but he was also unused to the dark and the lights of oncoming cars, which alarmed him. Thirty miles later, I was home, exhausted enough to allow Jochen to attend to the horse.

7 Berlin

$\mathcal{W}$hen Stefan was five years old, he got his first siege of bronchitis, which was soon followed by asthma. I believed it was physical, as did everyone else, and not till many years later did I become aware that the intense political atmosphere surrounding Stefan made him particularly prone to that illness. For Stefan, with his reddish blond hair, fiercely blue eyes, and light skin was more than normally sensitive. Nor was it just the political tension in Gross-Glienicke, which was no more than a mile from the English sector of Berlin. There was also the airlift when the access routes to East Berlin were cut off. Planes carrying supplies from the American sector zoomed loudly, regularly, and directly over our house, about three or four times a day. None of us liked that, but I know I became used to it, as did, apparently, Joel and most adults—but it, along with the almost continuous political discussions, could not help being especially unnerving—devastating?—to such a child.

Then both Joel and Stefan contracted slight cases of scarlatina—they could easily have been tended at home but there was a law which I was forced to obey: all contagious diseases, or illnesses requiring a quarantine, had to be hospitalized. So Joel and Stefan were driven to a hospital in Berlin, a hospital which housed contagious diseases in one section, which turned out to be a kind of barracks. There was another law: parents were not allowed to visit their children in the hospital—some official or officials had decided that mothers were hysterical, mothers only made matters worse for the children as well as the doctors and nurses. It was a law, and I had to obey it.

I remember peeking at both children through a window of the one-floor building, where I saw enough neglect to cause me to complain. That helped some, but only confirmed the official view that parents were a nuisance. So Bodo and I waited out the time for the quarantine to end, and then drove to the Berlin hospital to pick up the children. Joel, six years older than Stefan, came through all right, but that same night I realized that Stefan had a fever and that he had not been examined before leaving the hospital. Gross-Glienicke had no doctor, but Usch Gessner's brother from West Berlin was visiting her then. True, he had not yet graduated from medical school, but he was better than no doctor at all. Gerhard came, examined Stefan, and then called his doctor father in West Germany for consultation. It was determined that Stefan had contracted diphtheria—clearly while in the hospital where he had been confined. All night long, with calls going back and forth, Gerhard worked on Stefan, who, so near death, almost didn't mind the countless injections of penicillin. It was a horrible night, but he lived. (Some twenty years later I was to wish that he had died that night—and thus been saved from his lifelong pain and loneliness.) After weeks of recovery, a doctor from the Berlin hospital came, extremely solicitous, and obviously feeling culpability for a condition that originated in the hospital. He announced that the large doses of penicillin necessary to save Stefan's life had affected his heart, and recommended absolute bed rest, which he suggested might be most effectively secured in his hospital in Berlin. He proposed taking Stefan on as his private patient. Knowing nothing, not even enough of the language to argue, I acceded, believing the hospitalization necessary.

This time I could not even peek in a window, because Stefan was bedded somewhere on the fifth floor, and I could only phone and ask about his condition. I got nowhere, of course, mothers being not only hysterical but ignorant as well, so I had to wait out the two weeks. We arrived to pick up our son on the day he was to be discharged. A nurse dressed him. We found that the doctor was not around, but we learned of Stefan's forced bed rest and continuous crying before we drove him back with us to Gross-Glienicke.

Bodo and I saw that Stefan was unable to walk into the house. This disability was not just due to weakness from the length of time he had spent in bed. Stefan had become lame—an after-diphtheria lameness, we were told—so for almost six months he received regular physical-therapy treatments, until he was able to walk naturally again. It is impossible to know the effect this ordeal had on him.

During those first years, Berlin was more or less an open city, open in that, despite the borders between the different sectors—American, English, Russian, and French—one could move back and forth with relative ease and only a show of papers for the casual glance of the border guards. There were a sizable number of Berliners, therefore, who lived in the Russian sector but worked in West Berlin, and vice versa. But there was a difference in the currency, and those who worked in the West got paid in west marks. The exchange rate then was four east marks to one west mark. Consequently, everything in the East was one-fourth as expensive as in the West *if* one had Western currency. Of course there wasn't much to be had in the East, nor was the quality in most cases as good as in the West, but West Berliners who were unemployed, or poor, or simply liked bargains, bought regularly in the East. In the East, however, despite the relatively low quality and the lack of luxury items, there was no unemployment, and there was enough for everyone, certainly food and the necessities of everyday living. But with the increasing numbers of West Berliners buying in the East, supplies began to be depleted and there was a flourishing black-market exchange, and not a little resentment among East Berlin residents. An attempt was made at stricter controls: before making a purchase in the East one had to prove residency with an East German passport. But that restriction too proved easy to get around, and ineffective.

Music was an activity I was able to engage in without a knowledge of German. I learned how universal music is as a language through playing in a string orchestra in Potsdam. I could scarcely converse with the other players, but music and orchestral indications on a score are understandable in any language, so I had no difficulty. Jochen drove me to Potsdam for rehearsals. It was a professional orchestra, and we gave concerts regularly—I even earned some money. The German ritual before rehearsals was, to me, extraordinary. Germans are especially punctilious about shaking hands when meeting. But to meet for a rehearsal and have to shake the hand of each of the dozens of players was, for me, a challenge, since it was necessary to tuck my violin under the left arm and switch the bow to the left hand in order to accomplish it. No one else, however, seemed to find it as awkward as I, or as funny, for that matter.

But my two days a week of rehearsals were not enough for me—Bodo was usually busy, and Joel, outgoing as he was and occupied with his friends, seemed all right. Only Stefan, with his inexplicable attacks of bronchitis and recurring asthma, needed me. Still, I thought, perhaps once or twice a week I could ride with Bodo to Berlin if I was able to find some work in English.

I approached John Peet, an English journalist who had previously worked for Reuters in London. He had become disgusted and incensed when Reuters continued to change his copy from fact to half-truths and lies, and he eventually emigrated to East Germany. The German language was not a problem for him, since he had previously been married to an Austrian woman and had lived in Vienna. In East Berlin, John put out a four-page English-language paper, the *German Democratic Report.* He did it practically single-handedly, and neither had nor wanted help apart from a woman typist. One day I asked if I could be of use, possibly with proofreading, and I was pleased and excited by his affirmative answer.

And so I began traveling into Berlin with Bodo a few times a week. That was in the early fifties—a strangely tense and, in general, an oppressive time in East Germany. I was not much affected, concerned as I mainly was with my own personal life with Bodo and the two children. It was, nevertheless, impossible not to notice and even feel the tension.

There was a general sense of dissatisfaction, stemming from a strong dislike of the way the country was run, and everyone I knew or knew of disliked the head of the East German state, Walter Ulbricht. People were confused and angered by the conception, often expressed in the news, of the dictatorship of the proletariat. The workers simply did not feel that they had a say in anything, let alone deciding policy, and it only slightly appeased them to know that the officials of the government had been themselves members of the working class and were, supposedly, representing its interests. People did not feel represented, however, certainly not by Walter Ulbricht.

Of course, there were exceptions, and I think now of Horst Uhlen, the steelworker husband of a former maid of ours. Horst became a party member, and I remember the apartment where Lilo and Horst lived, with rows and rows of books, mainly political, including Karl Marx's *Das Kapital,* almost in shreds from rereading. Horst was genuine, and he believed, as Bodo for years did, in the possibility of a successful socialist Germany. Bodo and Horst were good friends, and spent hours together discussing problems and possible solutions. I liked the men's relationship, liked the idea of Bodo having a member of the working class as a friend, even if there was an element of tokenism in it.

The great majority of people in East Germany were not, I believe, dissat-

isfied with the idea of socialism. I doubt if most of the population would have
wanted a return to capitalism, or to a government like West Germany's. For
many, there was a kind of safety in socialism, even in the bare beginnings of
a socialist state. There was safety in the knowledge of full employment, cheap
apartments, food and work enough for everyone, free medical care, and paid
vacations. And I think if the general population had been allowed a fair vote,
the majority very probably would have opted for socialism—but with some
drastic changes, beginning with freedom of information and freedom to
travel. Naturally, it is impossible to know how Germany might have developed if there had not been a split between East and West and if there had not
been the Marshall Plan, which, while helping the West, made a kind of show-
case of West Berlin, a bright facade of buildings, with show windows full of
consumer goods not available in the East. West Berlin was a demonstration—a come-on—and with reason many thousands fled to the West, lured
by the promise which that brightness offered. Some were disappointed, but
many did find a fuller and more colorful life.

Since it was mainly the middle class which fled to the West, the eastern
part began to look more and more like a country of the working class and
professionals: writers, artists, engineers, doctors, and the like. There almost
ceased to be a middle class. The United States spent millions on sabo-
tage—for instance, an enormous espionage organization, called the Gehlen
network, funded with massive United States aid and headed by the former
chief of the Nazi secret service, was at work throughout the eastern bloc,
doing everything possible to subvert, halt, and delay production and to cause
as much damage as possible. But even apart from that, there was much to be
dissatisfied with in East Germany. The East German workers harbored an
intense dislike for the privileged class, and I know that many among the privileged—the intelligentsia in particular—were rankled by the class cleavage as
well. The intelligentsia were Communists, after all, and given to reflection,
and they were not comfortable with the division of classes and the consequent
inequality. There was, occasionally, an attempt to bridge this gap. Bodo
sometimes went to the countryside to factories and talked with the workers.
Once I went with him and watched. The manager, a brusque, good-natured
man who had fought in Spain and had spent two years in a concentration
camp, rounded up the workers, and they seemed to like Bodo. There was a
pleasant sense of camaraderie, but it is hard to tell what effect Bodo's discussion had. Perhaps the gap between intellectuals and workers was too wide to

be bridged, though I do remember workers being encouraged to write, and books by workers being welcomed and published. In general, however, I don't believe there was an adequate understanding between workers, peasants, and intellectuals.

Granted the obvious difficulties of trying to establish a socialist state among a disillusioned and war-torn population in a split country, there did seem to be a rigidity and an amazing lack of imagination in the effort. I was unable to understand, for instance, why the newspapers had to be so uniformly boring, with nothing of negative tenor allowed concerning the East. Nor could I understand why only negativity was evident in what little news there was of the West. The linkage of good with the East and evil with the West extended to literature and the arts. The lack of commodities, felt especially in the absence of variety in food, also made for a general dissatisfaction. Given, besides, the overall dreariness of the city's streets, the lack of adequate lighting, and yes, even the grim look of the people, it was easy to understand the urge to go to the West if at all possible. But the East had some advantages: no one had to go hungry or without work, medical needs were met by the state, and even higher education cost nothing. The free education, however, involved a large *but:* one could study practically anything and go in education as far as one liked, but the study of Marxism was a must, just as joining the youth movement was a must. In addition, the children of workers and Communists were given preference over the middle class, non-Communists, and business people. But if one was not too much of an individualist, and especially if one embraced the idea of socialism, there was a lot of good, and for everyone there was always the expectation that conditions would improve. For us, members of the intelligentsia, the privileged, life was not bad.

I had not been working long for John Peet when news came of arrests in other eastern countries—arrests of well-known Communists, even party officials. There were trials, and subsequent executions. There was, it seemed, a general suspicion of Communists who had spent years of exile from Hitler-dominated Germany and Europe anywhere but in the Soviet Union. There were accusations of bourgeois nationalism, Zionism, espionage for the West, and the like. The accused were all tried and true Communists, many had fought with the international brigade in Spain, and many were known to be Jewish.

One was not sure what to think, except that, of those we knew or knew of, it was unimaginable that they were traitors. But they confessed, and there were executions, hangings. I was with John Peet when the party newspaper, *Neues Deutschland,* published the confession of a friend of Bodo's and mine whom we had known well in Mexico before he went back to his native Czechoslovakia. André Simone was his pseudonym as a writer, but we had always known him as Otto Katz. Otto and his pleasant wife, Ilse, visited us frequently. I trusted my instincts, which told me, unequivocally, that Otto was no spy. He may not have been the most likable person I knew, but he was as committed a Communist as there was. I knew he could not have believed in or done what he was saying, in words that sounded just like him, in print. There was no doubt that the confession was his, and yet I could not believe it. John, I remember, was puzzled, but not at all as sure as I that Otto was innocent.

Otto was hanged, along with eleven others, including Slansky, the deputy premier of the Czech government, also Jewish. Ilse, I heard, was sent to the countryside, to work in a factory. Was I frightened? Was Bodo frightened? I don't remember feeling fear, but I knew, as I believe Bodo did, that something was very wrong. I was fully conscious that I was Jewish and that Bodo had been in exile in Mexico. But I felt secure enough, partly because it was all happening outside Germany. I had had no experience of anti-Semitism since I had come to Germany, and I was aware of the new, and very rigorous, East German law which punished severely the slightest anti-Semitic slur. There was a lot of talk among our friends, though, that was unnerving. Within Germany, however, I heard of no execution during that time. Arrests there were, but at least no one was hanged or shot.

Not long after, in June, I happened to be in Berlin, in John Peet's office, when the now-famous uprising occurred. John was busily doing paste-ups, and I was quietly reading some copy. When a long, distant rumbling reached the large rooms, which were up two flights and had a small balcony overlooking Friedrichstrasse, we both looked up simultaneously, but without alarm. I don't think the sound bothered John any more than it did me, until we realized that what we were hearing came from many, many people. The faint rumble turned less and less faint, and soon there was the unmistakable beat of hundreds of marching feet.

"Now what on earth is that?" John said, and we both got up as the typist came into the room. The three of us walked over and out the open glass doors onto the balcony.

The street below was empty, but farther down on the sidewalks, men were walking, three or four abreast, each with a lunch pail and most with a jacket slung over one shoulder. They were workers, out on strike, and the thought ran through my head, But this isn't right; workers don't strike in a socialist country. Yet, there they were, marching resolutely along in the middle of a sunny afternoon. Well, why shouldn't they? I left that question for later, intending to get my answer from Bodo—or did I already know the answer? This was a peasants and workers' state, and it was supposed to belong to them. So how could they strike? Does one strike against oneself? Then I remembered the production norms, and the stories I had been hearing. The norms were high and had recently had been made even higher, with no matching increase in pay. Peasants on the farms were not given enough by the state for their produce. Strict jail sentences were being imposed on anyone caught selling in the West.

We watched the men's purposeful stride as they approached Unter den Linden, and then something happened, and it was hard to tell why or what caused the sudden change. The men were no longer walking quietly on the sidewalks, with a few straggling in the street. They seemed to have moved as a body into the street—more and more of them—and they were becoming louder. Perhaps they had been joined by other marchers moving along Unter den Linden, which crossed Friedrichstrasse. But that could not have been the whole explanation, for what had been an obvious yet quiet action, a walking away from work, was now the purposeful advance of a more and more raucous crowd of men.

Then John began to yell down at them, in German, "Go on home! What do you think you're doing? These are your own factories! It's your country!"

A few looked up indifferently as they moved past, but I don't remember anyone's shouting a retort.

Then John had what he thought was a brainstorm. He went quickly back into his office, to a corner where an outsized red flag stood limply, reaching almost to the ceiling. He bent down for the flag's supporting pole and, using both hands, like Lancelot with his sword, moved out onto the balcony, where holding the staff he let the bright red banner drape down off the rail, and he continued his shouting: "Go home! You're striking against yourselves! This is your flag!"

The moving mass of men slowly came to a halt. Heads began to turn up to our balcony. It was then that John, suddenly alarmed, announced what I had neither heard nor noticed: "They're coming up! Lock the door!"

Some of the men had indeed entered the building and were climbing the stairs. As John backed in with the flag and placed it back in the corner, I ran to the door to lock it. I quite clearly heard the heavy tramping of men mounting the two flights. I still felt safe—wasn't the door locked? And it was a large steel door. There seemed to be little reason for concern. Shouts continued from the street below: "Throw down the flag!" "Give us that flag!" "Throw it down!" "We want that flag!" And then began the sound of banging against the locked door. "Open this door!" "We want the flag!"

John tried to reason through the locked door: "Go on home. This is your flag. You're workers, aren't you? And this is the workers' flag." The shouting continued below in the streets. Then the banging became organized. It was many bodies, in rhythm, throwing their entire weight against the door, over and over and over again.

Now I was frightened! I began to think solely of my two boys, Joel and Stefan, an hour and a half away in Gross-Glienicke, and to wish desperately to be there with them. Frightened I certainly was, but my thoughts, darting in all directions, did not envision any real disaster. I was simply scared, and felt completely trapped and helpless as I listened to the massive steel hinges gradually give way. I don't know what I expected, probably some form of bodily violence, but as I have learned many times since, nothing is ever quite what one expects.

The door crashed in, and six large men practically fell in with it. They righted themselves and walked determinedly in my direction. I don't remember seeing where John or the typist stood. I certainly expected to be struck down. But my presentiment was mistaken. One of the men pushed me roughly to one side; they all glanced at the now-empty balcony and around the room, and then moved to their destination—the flag in the corner.

The crowd below continued yelling, as one of the men upstairs grabbed the flag. While the rest looked on with evident satisfaction, he dropped it to the waiting, outstretched hands below. Then, brushing his palms together with a "That's taken care of" gesture, he walked out toward the stairs, the other men following. Not one of them bothered to look at or speak to us.

It is difficult to know what is true when one is being influenced. Am I being influenced now? And can I trust my present perceptions of events past, or even of events now? For it was easy for me then to believe that these men were Nazis: each of their faces seemed to have a peculiarly hard, cold, and mean expression that I had learned to identify with a Nazi. And when I was told later that "elements" from West Berlin had come over to the eastern part of the city, it seemed obvious that these were Nazi hoodlums from West Berlin who had been deliberately sent over to provoke decent workers to strike and riot. Yet, from where I am now, none of that seems so obvious. Might not the six men who forced the door down at John Peet's office have been simply East German workers outraged at what they saw as John's provocative gesture with the red flag—a gesture in direct defiance of all the injustices they were striking against? And the flag by that time symbolized for them those injustices. Doesn't anger or hatred distort the features of any face? I also remember seeing, as the men marched by, some raised fists, in the traditional manner of striking workers all over the world. This gesture, although in defiance of the government, was not necessarily a wholesale rejection of it. Whatever the truth, and whatever changed the strike into a riot, a riot there was.

The men below our balcony set about making a bonfire, and the flag was burned to ashes in the middle of the street. I don't remember hearing or seeing any particular jubilation over that. The crowd began to thin and to move on—as a Russian tank approached along Unter den Linden. It moved slowly, turned, and then inched its way up Friedrichstrasse, clearing the streets. A Russian officer's head appeared from the turret. The thought occurred that either he was fearless or there was little danger, since he didn't seem at all perturbed. It was then that I realized that there was not a policeman in sight.

I was alone with the typist, waiting for Bodo, who had called and promised to be over in minutes. He was on Französische Strasse, which wasn't far away. John had disappeared—to join Georgia, his bride-to-be, and they both spent the rest of the afternoon trying to argue and reason with groups of people in the streets. It was a brave gesture, because people were on a rampage, overturning cars when they could and generally venting their rage. The absence of the Volkspolizei was, I learned, the result of an official order, and it turned out to be a blessing. The presence of police on the streets would certainly have resulted in bitter confrontations and further violence. As it was, I did hear sporadic shots, perhaps four or five in all. The total number of people shot varies, of course, with the side of the border on which the figures were calculated, since the West was as ready to inflate the number killed as the authorities in the East were to minimize it.

The typist had already left when Bodo arrived with Jochen, and the three of us set off for home. I had never before minded that long route around West Berlin, but it seemed interminable now that I was afraid for Joel's and Stefan's safety. And I thought of how simple it used to be, before there was a border dividing East and West Berlin. I kept my bitter thoughts and anxiety to my-self, however, and tried to listen to Bodo and Jochen discuss the events of the afternoon.

Jochen was sympathetic with the construction workers who had begun the strike: the production quotas were much too high, the situation simply unbearable. Bodo, though not unsympathetic, seemed more disturbed by the negligence of the government, which had brought the workers to the breaking point. He spoke of economic difficulties and the need for more consumer goods. Word of the strike, apparently, had begun spontaneously, then had spread like wildfire. Workers from the suburbs had joined in, as had men and boys from West Berlin, motivated, Jochen suggested, by an interest in causing as much damage as possible. Bodo spoke further of economic troubles and the necessity of preserving socialist Germany at all costs—his view being that West Germany was a hotbed of not so latent Nazism and militarism. He was pleased that the East German authorities had had the foresight to keep the Volkspolizei off the streets, for confrontations with the police might have resulted in enough violence to bring American tanks into the East. The tanks, at the ready on the border, would have come in, ostensibly to bring order, but actually to crush the socialist government and possibly unify the two Germanys. That, said Bodo, would have almost certainly led to open war, since the Soviet tanks, equally ready, would never have conceded socialist Germany.

When we arrived home, Stefan was already asleep, but Joel, obviously relieved to see us, had a wide-eyed tale to relate of hundreds of Russian tanks moving endlessly up Potsdamer Chaussee on the way to Berlin, causing a trembling of the earth that could be felt at least a mile around. "They just didn't stop going by," he said, and the tanks were still moving along when he finally became too tired to watch and came home to wait for us.

Six years later, while Joel was working in the little seaport town of War-nemünde, one of the workers there talked of the June 17 uprising, and told Joel how some of the men then, hearing of the Berlin trouble, had promptly hoisted a Nazi flag. Today I remember the raised fists of the strikers on Fried-richstrasse, the faces of the six men who broke down our door, and Joel's story of the Nazi flag—and I also remember Bodo, a dedicated Communist and a good man. These are fragments of memories, complex and contradic-tory, which seem to form pieces of a puzzle: a puzzle quite possibly not to be solved.

Some months later in 1953, I went to the Soviet Union with Stefan. His bronchial asthma attacks were becoming more and more frequent—and it seemed he was at home, sick, more than in school. He had no friends, mainly because of his bouts of sickness, and I spent most of the time with him, playing games with little toy cars on the floor, trying to make myself into the playmate he needed, or supplying him, while he was laid up, with reams of blank paper to make his drawings: strangely advanced drawings for his age, satirical depictions of the life around him. The doctors were unanimous in seeing a climate change as the only solution—"salt sea air," said one, "mountain air," said another—but in my mind everything seemed to point to another country entirely, and I secretly hoped for a miracle, something which would find us all out of Germany, away from the weeks of cloudy days. Of course, I yearned for America as the solution, but my yearning was scarcely allowed to reach consciousness, since I knew its unreality. I was not able to imagine Bodo in the United States. And none of my yearnings and secret hopes were as powerful as the prayer that we, the four of us, might stay well and together, wherever.

I think I surprised Bodo by my readiness to go alone with Stefan to the Soviet Union, for I knew no Russian and only enough German by then to "get along." I see this now as yet another example of my lifelong tendency to forge ahead, without much thought, to take chances and risks in a kind of intuitive belief in a satisfactory outcome. Our stay was to be for three months and was arranged by invitation as a "cure" to be accomplished at a resort in the Caucasus. It seemed logical that I should go—and unthinkable for Bodo to be away that long from his work and activities in Berlin.

I remember my excitement as the plane we were on began flying over Soviet territory, and I pointed out to Stefan, trying to infect him with my own enthusiasm, how different the socialist countryside looked—miles and miles of unbroken fields, since there were no longer any private estates.

Stefan and I were important guests, the wife and son of a well-known German writer and Communist, and we were treated accordingly. A large black official car met us at the airport in Moscow and took us about. We were given rubles to spend, and a suite at an elegant hotel with marble halls, wide, curved staircases, and crystal chandeliers. We were taken to every event of note that November in the capital. And the Russians, always mindful of the wishes and needs of children, also took us to the circus, to mime shows, and to puppet shows. After two weeks of being feted in that style, we flew to the sanatorium in the Caucasus where Stefan was to receive special care for his asthma. There too we had a suite, with a little balcony on which I could lie in the sun. Although it was winter, the temperature, I remember, was exceedingly high—yet so very dry that one scarcely felt uncomfortable. On a table in our little sitting room was a bowl of fresh fruit, and it always looked fresh and appetizing, because the maid who kept the rooms clean changed and rearranged it daily, removing and replacing any grapes, apples, or bananas even slightly beyond their prime.

Was Stefan as lonely as I? He had a routine, which was part of his cure, and there were hours on end of our playing together—there being no other children. If he was not lonely, I believe that that was the result of my own determination that he not be so, as I played with considerable success the part of another eight-year-old. We had only each other for two full months, because no one except the interpreter assigned to us spoke either English or German. And the interpreter, a middle-aged woman named Victoria, spoke no English, and her German was not much better than my own. Victoria, it turned out, was not only extremely dull, but downright mean, particularly on realizing—as she did almost immediately—that her power over us was supreme: she could say anything, or withhold anything, and there was no recourse. How can one have recourse in a language no one else understands? I kept from Stefan my own awareness that Victoria's behavior was prompted by hatred—possibly because I was American, or the wife of a German—and by her obvious delight at having free scope for her sadism, for instance, in putting ground hot pepper on the nose of a cat Stefan and I had befriended. She laughed contentedly when we reacted with horror and outrage. And she pretended we were not allowed to eat anywhere but alone in our rooms, which added to our loneliness. She also placidly withheld from us information about English-language entertainment that I eventually discovered was available.

Away from the sanatorium there were, however, some high points of interest and even amusement. We watched a handsome man of middle years, a large camera and tripod strapped to his back, descend one of the many steep hills. He had the blackest and largest handlebar moustache I had ever seen: it grew inches beyond either side of his face, the tips carefully groomed and pointing upward. I would have loved a picture of him, but instead he took a picture of Stefan and me. We had to stand very still in front of a large boulder until he was ready to snap, and he waited for other customers before trudging back up the hill. I enjoyed our walks too, and was intrigued by the

Russian habit of walking slowly along, head bent, to pore over a book. Our walks around the sanatorium took us past dreary-looking hovels, most without electricity, and occasionally past the work-worn face of a peasant drawing water from a hand-pumped well. Except for an occasional glance from people in the sanatorium, well-dressed government people or their families, no one showed any interest in us, and without their language we found it impossible to do more than offer a hello.

Still, I think Stefan enjoyed the time there even though there were no other children. He had a routine; there were no tensions or discussions he could not understand. He was well during the entire two months—a record—and as the only child he received very special attention and care, much different from what he was accustomed to in Germany.

The usual Russian sensitivity to and love of children was not new to me. I had noticed it with Russian soldiers in Germany—a simple, natural, and straightforward friendliness, unconstrained by the presence of any accompanying adult. That was quite the opposite of the German manner with children. Germans were apt to require good behavior of all children older than two or three years, even other people's, and in the main I was shocked by the patronizing, condescending attitude of adults toward them—a blatant lack of imagination and an unwillingness to think of themselves as ever having been children. Russians, on the other hand, seemed to have a natural understanding of children. In my memory there is a large Russian soldier in a badly fitting uniform, his cap almost falling off the back of his head, revealing his shock of uncombed hair, and his homely face beaming as he bends forward and beckons to a small child not his own. It is in a streetcar, and the rest of the passengers, all German, look on in a combination of distaste and disapproval. But there is perfect accord between the child and the Russian, who, intent on the child, is unaware of those around.

Lonely as I had been in the Soviet Union, I did not look forward to going home to Gross-Glienicke: all of the friends we had been accustomed to spending time with had already moved to Berlin. When the eastern section of Germany was formally declared a sovereign state, the division between East and West was absolute, or at least as close to absolute as possible. It was no longer simple to go back and forth between East and West Germany, and the border guards, especially those in the East, were thorough in their examination of bags and parcels, though there was smuggling going on in both directions. The elderly German woman who lived across the street from us in Gross-

Glienicke kept chickens and regularly carried her eggs across the border to sell for west marks.

With the closing of access routes, we could no longer go to Berlin the short way, through the West. Consequently, those of our friends who worked in East Berlin began to move into the city—and I had become isolated, what with Bodo mainly busy in Berlin and Joel away at school in Potsdam.

Our decision to move to Berlin, too, required coming to terms with what to do with Roland, my horse. Roland, not quite ten years old, had been treated with love and care since his arrival at our place in Gross-Glienicke. He was spoiled as a horse rarely is, and I was determined that he not go the way of most horses. I certainly did not want to sell him, and I knew that giving him to a friend carried no assurance that the friend would keep him. My problem was solved by presenting him to the Berlin Zoo. I still have the formal certificate, which looks somewhat like a diploma: it has the zoo's seal and is signed by the director, who assured me that Roland would not be sold during his lifetime and would be used for only light work. I believe anyone who has ever loved a horse, or horses, for that matter, will understand me on this score, and understand as well how one can be drawn to an animal so lacking in, say, the more obvious intelligence of a dog, and why, even now, I am almost irresistibly drawn to and take pleasure in the smell of a stable and horses.

It was interesting and fun getting our house in Berlin together. It was one of a group of houses allotted to writers, painters, and sculptors in a special artists' colony, all new though not well built. Most of our friends lived in more or less identical houses nearby, or else in somewhat more pretentious houses which had previously been owned by well-to-do Germans, either Nazis or Jews who had fled Germany.

Our house had a large atelier, which we used for a living room—an immense space with windows onto the street, a large skylight, and a large tile oven in one corner for additional warmth during the hard Berlin winters. The tile oven was the most efficient source of heat in the entire house—far superior to the cellar furnace—probably because the only coal available was briquettes made for ovens rather than furnaces. Central heating was unheard of—or at least, I hadn't heard of it. At any rate, the atelier–living room was always comfortable, and by far the cheeriest room in the house.

I looked forward to a fuller life in Berlin, without, however, having any concrete idea of what that might consist in. There were friends around us, people of like mind and interests who were part of the intelligentsia and the professions. Crista Cremer and her husband, Fritz, lived nearby in a house similar to ours. Fritz was a devoted Communist and a good sculptor, serious and likable; his face looked as though it were chiseled out of granite. He loved Crista, also a talented sculptor, and a good mother to her three children. Crista's graceful body is often seen in Fritz's sculptures. Heintz Kamnitzer, another neighbor, taught history at Humboldt University. His wife, Irene, had been a successful actress in West Germany and had left a career for Heintz. It meant that Heintz, who loved his wife dearly, spent much of his life trying to find an acting niche for her. She eventually became hopelessly bored and frustrated and began to drink heavily. Then there was the sculptor and painter René Graetz and his lovely and humorous Irish wife, Elizabeth Shaw, a good and successful cartoonist. There were interesting, sometimes even gay, times at the Presseklub, a restaurant and bar for journalists and writers where we ate and met with friends. Occasionally we got together with Bertolt Brecht and his wife, the actress Helene Weigel, at the Möwe, a restaurant frequented by theater people. Especially after a performance the discussions were animated and sparkling. Bodo, I remember, liked exchanging detective novels with Brecht.

Stefan Hermlin was perhaps Bodo's closest colleague and friend. Hermlin, with his classic, handsome face, and never without his pipe, was a good if not very productive poet who went through a succession of pretty wives and received an annual salary from Bodo's magazine, for which he did nothing. When an occasional piece or poem did appear, he was paid handsomely, an arrangement I had difficulty understanding. Nevertheless, I liked and felt myself liked by Stefan. The Eisler brothers, Gerhard and Hanns, lived nearby, in separate houses, with their wives. I did not particularly like Gerhard, a clever politician, who with his wife, Hilde, had spent his years of exile in the United States and, then, during the McCarthy years, had as a wanted Communist slipped away and escaped on a Polish boat, to settle in Germany. Hilde came soon after, and I can still see her as she spoke before a small gathering at Berlin's Newspaper Press Club—her eyes filling with tears until she broke down, telling of her return to find her entire family murdered by the Nazis. Hanns and Gerhard played chess together, once a week, tensely, judging by my own memory of one evening playing Ping-Pong with Gerhard in Gross-Glienicke. He played a good game, but I played a better, and after three successive losses he refused to stop, though I had had enough and so had others who had been watching. Gerhard was determined to win before he quit. True, I played my best, and played to win, but I shall never forget Gerhard's frenzy and his insistence that we continue, until it was past three in the morning and he finally did beat me. I was earnest then about continuing to win—just as I am now about losing, and have been for years, when an opponent shows such a need to win.

It was Bodo who got me work at the Berlin radio station. I had been depressed ever since the overseas call had come telling of Jim's sudden death, in a taxi, on the way to a doctor. Jim and I had been corresponding—and I was looking forward to his trip to Europe to see us. He had plans of doing a movie with John Huston, and he was going to visit us then. He had barely mentioned his heart problems. The news of his death was a complete shock. Joel too was saddened, though he had had too little contact with his father to experience the death as a deep loss. I remember his bitter remark the day after we heard the news: "Well, I guess there's no reason for me to go to the United States now." I became desperate for something to do. I wanted to get my mind off Jim, and to be busy during the day. Except for Joel and Stefan, who were mostly at school, nothing and no one needed me, and housework, even cooking when I did not feel like it, was done by a live-in maid. I was bursting with energy and the need for activity, and I daydreamed about the pleasure of constructing something, a house maybe. It was during that time that I took to digging up heavy shovelfuls of some fifteen square yards of our backyard. I had thoughts of a vegetable garden, which we didn't need, and a strawberry patch. After that, Bodo, aware of my plight, asked me to type out a small notebook he had found in Spain. Partly in Spanish and French, with some English, it turned out to be the diary of a young homosexual of the Spanish royal family, who, from what I could make out, was pouring out his loves and daily troubles to ease his own pain and boredom. I soon tired of the task: it wasn't something really necessary. Then Bodo talked with someone at the radio station, and I began to apply myself to an assignment which might get me hired by the English-speaking radio of Berlin. I was hired, even got a salary, and was provided with a desk—which at once made me feel important and useful. I worked hard, thought up ideas for the programs— feature stories, most of which were accepted—and soon I was a regular. Whenever anyone of importance was visiting the country, I interviewed him or her over the radio, always live: Diego Rivera, Pablo Neruda, the Dutch documentary filmmaker Joris Ivens, others of equal fame, and some less well known.

The interviews went easily for me, since most of the visitors were good friends of Bodo's and seemed to like me. It was Bodo's status too that gave me the confidence that overcame my normal shyness and sense of inadequacy, for I realized, almost from the start of my years in East Germany, that being the wife of a well-known and active writer did wonders for my ego. The magic words *Frau Uhse* seemed to open doors automatically. I felt as though I did not have to do or be anything on my own, nor, I suspected, did it matter what I looked like. Some years earlier, as Jim's wife, I had experienced how being good-looking could help in overcoming inadequacies, but then it was expected of wives in general, certainly during my New York years, that they be pretty and reasonably intelligent, but never forward or overly ambitious.

When Diego Rivera arrived from the Soviet Union to visit East Germany, I was selected to take him on a tour of the *Rundfunk,* or radio station, possibly because I had known him in Mexico and spoke Spanish. Two portions of the tour stand out. Diego pointed to a large space on one of the outside walls of the station and remarked that it needed something—a mural perhaps. I asked if he would consider painting one, immediately thinking of how it would enhance my personal prestige if I could get him to agree. He promised to return with helpers, but he never did. The second memory takes me to a small balcony where an official of the station was explaining some newly acquired piece of equipment. Diego, some feet away, looked at neither the machine nor the official, however. His bulging eyes were riveted instead on an open magazine on a nearby table: the large art photograph of a naked woman had his undivided attention.

That evening, Bodo and I gave a little reception for the artist, inviting people who spoke either English or Spanish. It seemed to me that Rivera was overcareful about extolling the virtues of the Soviet Union and the German Democratic Republic. It was understood that pilgrims to the socialist countries, and particularly to the Soviet Union, would return with glowing accounts of the progress evident and the robust health of the people. There was always enthusiastic praise for increases in production and in the availability of goods. Much of this was true. Progress was conspicuous: newly constructed buildings, more apartment houses, more consumer goods. But criticism was invariably sparing. All deficiencies—the lack of supplies, inadequate housing, shortages in basic necessities—were attributed to growing pains. When a larger mistake was noticed, it was ascribed to the "birth pains of socialism." Visitors were shown the positives: the free medical care, the inexpensive housing and basic foods, the full employment. Socialism was, after all, relatively young and still in the stages of learning and growth. I absorbed the general certainty that "everything is getting better," that capitalism was rotten and dying, while socialism was vibrant and gaining—a new way, a cleaner way, where people interested in the common good worked for one another rather than for themselves.

I believed it all—believed *in* it and was even interested enough to try reading some Marx. More accessible, however, was a small volume by Lenin called *State and Revolution;* the idea Lenin expounded of a future without government, when the state naturally "withered away," was particularly appealing to me. My reaction was probably the harbinger of my present distrust of governments. There was also a gigantic official book *The History of the Revolution of the Union of Soviet Republics—Short Form.* No one else seemed to find it funny that it should be called short. I had almost completed skipping through it when it was declared obsolete, out-of-date, and unsuitable to be read. That was after Khrushchev had revealed the extent of Stalin's crimes to the Twentieth Party Congress. As in the case of other political upsets that occurred during those years, the shock everyone was experiencing was felt by me pretty much vicariously. I was neither a Communist nor an intellectual, with nothing like the stake in the party, in Stalin, or in Germany, for that matter, of those around me. They were thoroughly and deeply shocked, even grieved by Khrushchev's disclosures. Bodo, of course, was stunned, and I believe he never quite recovered, never quite believed again in the party's infallibility.

In the years since I left East Germany, I have been asked repeatedly what it was like to live there. I have varied the answers, depending on the questioner and the circumstances. Particularly during the closing years of the McCarthy era I altered my answers according to the political stance of my interrogator, sometimes unsure whether it was safe to speak openly. There have, of course, also been changes in my views. More and more I have come to see the complexities of almost every question.

Some time after Rivera's visit, I thought of writing an article for a magazine, on the "big three" of Mexican fresco painters: Diego Rivera, David Siqueiros, and José Clemente Orozco. I knew the editor of the only popular magazine in the East, and she was pleased with the idea of running the piece. I was proud of what I produced, and particularly gratified when Bodo and writer friends of ours not only liked it, but found no changes necessary. So I was baffled when Hilde Eisler, the editor of the magazine, told me it could not be published as it stood. I had given Rivera, who was then in high favor with the party, less space than Orozco or Siqueiros, and had even shown my preference for Orozco, giving him an extra paragraph. Of course, I objected, but when the article appeared, I was dismayed to see obliterated almost all the praise and admiration I had voiced for Orozco. Taken out as well was a slight negative observation concerning Rivera's work. Thus the final piece had the officially desired bias. It is not that the newspapers in the United States do not distort the news, but my experience in East Germany reflected a much larger and more pervasive, centrally controlled censorship. Sometimes I tried to understand the reasons behind it, as the writers themselves conceived them. I had to ask myself why they submitted to the conditions the government imposed on them. Often I heard them say that opening the doors wide to criticism and discussion would be playing into the hands of the enemy, that dirty laundry should not be displayed, that successes should be glorified and failures set right in silence. The idea was that freely available information would be ammunition for the enemy, namely, fascism. But Bodo, I know, felt uneasy with most of those explanations—and I know I occasionally expressed my misgivings to him: "Why can't you, and those like you, be trusted to say anything you like or feel? You are genuine and true Communists—and you would never say or write anything which would be harmful. You would tell the truth, good and bad, and you would be believed and trusted, and people would read your books and know the truth. It is all around them in any case." On those occasions, Bodo listened, but I don't remember his reply, if any. I only know he continued to write, not of the present, but only of events and people long dead.

In the daily papers, everything was presented so rosily that one would have thought there was no struggle at all, that there was no crime or social difficulty, that building socialism was a breeze, that it went quickly and smoothly forward as on ball bearings. Nobody believed that. All one had to do was be alive and look around. Progress there certainly was, but the newspapers went overboard about any slight gain, and never mentioned the reverses.

There were three days at the time of the Hungarian uprising in 1956 that were for me the most ominous and unsettling period I was to live through in Germany. That, I believe, was probably due to no one's really knowing what was happening. East German news always came in a form acceptable to offi-

cial circles, so for the first two days we heard little about the uprising except
what was transmitted almost nonstop by broadcasters in West Berlin. In the
East, there was a virtual silence until the party got its bearings, that is to say,
until it knew how things would turn out, after the Russians moved into
Prague. During those days we held our breath. Would there be uprisings all
through the eastern countries? Would there be a chain reaction? And if so,
what would that mean? Almost certainly total war, we presumed, since the
Russians would never tolerate a United Nations intervention in any of the
satellites.

Bodo was thoroughly frightened. He feared an invasion of East Germany
from the West, and his own certain capture by West German fascists. Bodo
anticipated torture. His fright was genuine, and he urged me to leave with the
children. Perhaps I was also scared, but I knew I couldn't leave him alone. I
was ready to send both Joel and Stefan—tags about their necks—to a friend
of Bodo's in West Berlin who would get them off to America. I was convinced
that Bodo should not be alone, that he needed me. Then Joel discovered a
bottle of ether and a jar containing wads of cotton in Bodo's desk. When
confronted, Bodo confessed that he had planned, in the event of a take-over
or uprising, to kill the children and me as well as himself. I was horrified and
can still see myself, alone in our backyard, digging a hole as deep as I could
manage and burying the ether and cotton. Shortly afterward, probably the
next day, when I went to a beauty shop—I had started having my hair
dyed—the eyes around me were suspicious, questioning, and accusing. I belonged to the intelligentsia—the privileged class—and the memory of the
attitude of others toward us during that time is still very alive in me.

The bloody days of the Hungarian uprising and the Russian invasion
were vividly shown in photographs in our papers. The atrocities, the papers
reported, were committed by fascists and by hoodlums incited by the West. I
have no doubt that there were some fascists, and hoodlums as well, and that
both groups received at least some support from the West. The part the western powers played—Radio Free Europe, for example—is now known. They
poured oil on the fire, encouraging the uprising. But I also have no doubt that
there was ample reason for the discontent that led to the uprising in the first
place, and that the government was repressive in the extreme. Anyway, the
Russians invaded, and the uprising was put down. Bodo published an article
in his magazine, *Aufbau,* by the well-known Czechoslovak intellectual and
Communist Georg Lukács—an article which spoke out in favor of Nagy's

transitional government and in support of certain reforms. Lukács, later in disfavor with the party, was arrested for a while, and Bodo was severely criticized. The magazine folded soon afterward, but whether the article contributed to its closure was never clear. Bodo, in any case, eventually became editor in chief of another influential magazine, *Sinn und Form*.

My work at the radio and television stations began to be more and more irregular as Stefan's bouts of asthma increased. I became convinced that he needed another change of climate, and Bodo and I began to talk of Mexico. Suddenly it became possible for Stefan and me to fly there and remain for a few months. I had my German passport, still with "good for ten years" stamped across my face, and flying KLM to Canada and straight down into Mexico without a stop on United States territory meant comparative safety. We left on a Czech plane, arriving in Amsterdam an hour before KLM was to take us to Canada and on to Mexico. We had scarcely left the Czech plane when an unknown young man carrying a large bunch of gladioli came over to me, introduced himself, and handed me the flowers, and Stefan a book. His affable manner had me completely confused. But when he began to talk and especially to question me—"Are you sure you want your son to grow up in that part of Germany?"—I realized he was an FBI agent. Stefan remained quiet throughout, our exchanges were for the most part polite, and I tried not to show surprise that he knew so much about my life—as, for example, that Bodo, on the same weekend, was in India, and that I was on my way to Mexico to stay in the house of friends whose daughter had studied to become an engineer in East Germany, since her profession was one girls could not train for in Mexico. The agent knew so much that I became distressed. Finally, when the hour's layover was ending, I insisted, "No, thank you," and gratefully boarded the plane for Mexico City. I rid myself of the gladioli, but Stefan kept his book, a copy of *Huckleberry Finn*.

The stay in Mexico accomplished for Stefan what I hoped and somehow knew it would. He remained free of attacks, gained weight, and became more outgoing and free. I remember powerful and painful wishes for the impossible—that somehow Bodo and Joel could come, that we could all be together in Mexico.

Stefan and I returned to Germany by the identical route—over the United States and on to Amsterdam to wait for the Czech plane to take us on to the East German republic. And there he was, in Amsterdam, the same agent, looking as affable as he had a few months before. We greeted each other automatically like old family friends. Luckily there was less time between planes this time, and he had only time to reiterate his main questions and perhaps hope that I might, some day, have a change of heart. I was glad when it was finally time to board the plane for Berlin, and Stefan was too.

Soon after Mexico, Bodo was to go to Paris on an official trip for the PEN Club, and it was decided that I could go along with him. I think now of that trip as marking the end of our relationship, and as presenting an example of one way at least in which I failed to understand the depth of Bodo's despair. Despair afflicted Bodo because he had never recovered from Khrushchev's denunciation of Stalin, and from the realization that he, believing in the party, had inadvertently had a part in an immense crime against the very good and hope he had always assumed the party stood for. He was further embittered by his inability to express himself freely, always writing "für die Schublade," for the desk drawer, as he said. His writing was now always of heroic events and people of the past. He could not write of the present and how it was, good and bad, because censorship required that anything about the present, factual or fictitious, show it in a rosy light and as having no flaws. Bodo was becoming more and more bitter and the overall atmosphere was oppressive.

Once in Paris, Bodo seemed like a changed man. "I love this city. I feel at home here," he told me. I did not realize the significance of those words then—that Bodo, normally so reticent, was expressing nostalgia for the years he had spent in Paris, before Spain and before going to the United States. It was in Paris that Bodo first experienced the fresh air of freedom after escaping Hitler's police, and it was Paris that brought out the natural bohemian spirit he kept in check in his native Germany. It had been a happy time, full of easy talk with friends, rich with work and hope.

Bodo spoke French and knew Paris. I, knowing little of the language and the city, was content simply to walk around while Bodo went to his meetings and, more important, visited and talked with his friend Louis Aragon. I think, however, that our main point of difference lay in my worry over Stefan, whose attacks had begun again after our return from Mexico. I had left him in the care of a maid, and my worries over his well-being spilled over onto Bodo and his newfound, if temporary, happiness. When I called East Berlin and discovered that Stefan was, indeed, ill again, I wanted badly to cut our visit short and return. Bodo acquiesced, but with evident pain and reluctance.

I mark the Paris trip as the beginning of Bodo's and my end, too, because shortly after our return, Bodo met and became involved with a woman—Frau

Wertzlau—and the following two years were as wretched as any I remember in my life, with the exception of those in the United States after leaving Germany, when I was trying to help Stefan, hoping he would not—"Oh please, God, don't let him"—kill himself. The pain, and the low periods, in one's life can only, I have learned, be judged by what one has suffered before. The loss of a job or money, excess weight, a car accident—each can seem, and be, of major importance and a terrible experience if nothing worse has happened before. An adolescent with acne, suffering agony before a dance, is usually judged with a tolerant smile, but the pain is as real as anything he or she has ever known.

If Bodo's involvement had been merely an extramarital affair, perhaps much of the ensuing disaster could have been avoided—but there was so much more. The ingredients which made up the disaster included, naturally, much of what had been wrong all along with Bodo's and my relationship—a relatively sexless marriage. On Bodo's side, therefore, a hunger existed to be loved and needed in that way. But she also came into his life at a particularly sensitive time, a time of bitter disillusion and political troubles as well as one in which he felt a general personal sense of collapse before having sufficiently lived, for he was in his middle fifties. And so he fell, heavily; nor does it matter that she was not worthy of him. That she was German may or may not have made a difference to him, but I remember my conviction, at the time, that that was important. I do not want to sound self-serving when I say that she was not worthy of him. In a sense she was, in that she could give him much that he was lacking then and dull some of the pain and bitterness of his political life. Naturally I fought back, seeing immediately the threat to myself. And I resented the hours, days, and yes, weeks alone with Stefan and his illness.

I watched Bodo's gradual deterioration. Always a drinker and chain smoker, he began looking slack and slovenly when he was home. From where I am now, and feel now, it is hard to remember and recognize myself as I was and behaved during that time. True, I was outraged and hurt, but I was completely devoid of pity or compassion for suffering outside my own. I was aware of Stefan's loneliness and pain, but I know I was too full of my own fury and outrage to help him much. Joel I know I used as a companion and sounding board for my own self-righteous complaints.

Despite the almost continuous fighting when we were together, Bodo and I made an attempt at a kind of life, and we seemed to feel better among friends with whom we could put on an act. One of the friends, a married artist who I knew had previously found me attractive, somehow recognized the extent of my vulnerability and did what he would never have tried before: he began to show up when Bodo was away. I eventually let myself be drawn into a relationship—mostly, I now realize, to keep my own head above water.

But Bodo's and my personal lives continued to flounder. I remember myself as mainly outraged, and even shocked, at the intensity and persistence of his drive toward a woman of whom I had heard nothing good. He seemed ready to leave not only me, but Joel and Stefan, for a life with her. There was some respite, of course. I began to practice my viola in earnest, daily and for hours at a time, in preparation for a concert (viola, voice, and piano), and after the concert I remember realizing that I had never played as well, and I felt the glow of success. What were particularly strange were the words that I overheard afterward: "That was Alma's swan song." The words were strangely prophetic, but how did he know, and what prompted his words?

Mostly, however, those many months were continuously downhill. Never much interested in food, I found myself unable to eat anything. I began to fear the rapid loss of weight, and vain as usual, came to mind the scrawny look of my face and neck. To keep up some semblance of strength, I began taking cod-liver-oil pills and drinking heavy cream poured into glasses of milk. Once, in Leipzig, where I had gone by train to meet my artist friend, I ordered a glass of milk and buttered toast, praying that I could down at least some of the toast. I couldn't, and that night, waiting in my hotel room, I began talking aloud to myself in a kind of stupor, just bits or parts of sentences, which I vaguely listened to: "I am going to leave Germany—Stefan and Joel—I haven't been there for twenty years—I am alone—I don't know anyone anymore—I am alone—I have no skills to sell—have never had a job—do I love Germany?—I am going to leave Germany—I will never see Usch again—I will never see anyone I now love again—I am going to Mexico first—for Stefan—I cannot work in Mexico—maybe I can, but what?—I will go to the States—I cannot kill myself—I have two children—I am alone— Stefan and Joel need me." It went on and on, until I finally dozed off.

It wasn't simply that my husband was in love with another woman. That, it is true, was disagreeable, as was the fact that I was very far from home ground—America. What eventually tipped the scales and caused a violent upheaval was Frau Wertzlau's pregnancy and her insistence on keeping the baby. There I balked, knowing instinctively that such a situation would make any further life with Bodo more than a little problematic. I presented Bodo with an ultimatum: either she gets an abortion or I leave the country for America, with Joel and Stefan. I had nothing of the sympathy then that I have now for Bodo's predicament. He loved his family, and didn't want to lose us, but neither could he face the loss of the woman with whom he was in love. His efforts, however, both money and pleas, for her to get an abortion were of no avail. She was determined to keep the baby, and eventually the child was born, in Leipzig.

I was outraged, and also desperate, and I bombarded Bodo with every-thing I could think of to increase his guilt: had I not aborted a baby, just a few years ago, because of him—and now, a baby by another woman—and was I not ready to send my children to the United States, alone, so that I could remain with him during the Hungarian uprising? My fury at his be-trayal was too vast for even self-pity, and I certainly had none for Bodo, whose suffering must have been acute.

The reserve of strength I must have had then certainly did not come from food, because I remained unable to swallow anything except liquids. My hair was coming out so rapidly that I remember the sight of my bathtub covered with strands of long dark brown hair. I began to make plans for returning to America, beginning with a call to a friend in Mexico: "I'm leaving Germany. It will take a few months. Can I send Stefan to you alone, right away, to stay until Joel and I arrive?" I yelled it all into the mouthpiece—connections were not yet that good—but I got an affirmative answer, and two weeks later Ste-fan was on his way. I see him now, not quite thirteen years old, walking ahead toward the transatlantic plane which would fly him to New York and on to Mexico, where my friend would meet him. A shoulder bag weighed him down as he walked as quickly as he could toward the plane, and he did not look back.

Next I called Joel, who had begun work in the shipyards at Warnemünde, probably to escape the mess at home. I wanted him back to help me with the plans, to be with me.

I must have moved through the following six weeks as in a dream, and I only vaguely remember the attempts of friends, mainly Usch, to persuade me to remain in Germany. For the most part, however, the days are blocked out of my memory, except for the day before our departure. Anna Seghers came that afternoon to say good-bye—she was not able, she said, to come to the train the next day. Others came too, but mainly I remember that evening, which began with a call from Frau Wertzlau, possibly prompted by Bodo, asking me to stay, not to leave Germany. She said that she was ready to give Bodo up. She asked me to meet with her. I had never met her, and certainly was not interested in doing so then. It was all too late; I was in motion to leave.

Bodo was home, looking ghastly and asking me repeatedly to change plans, and to bring Stefan back. I was unmoved. Then, later, from the bedroom, he called me—it was toward evening. I went and saw him standing by the dresser, a glass of water in one hand and in the other a fistful of pills. I did not know what kind. He began putting one after the other in his mouth, all the time looking at me, his expression fully defiant. Feeling suddenly strong, I looked back at him and heard my voice, hard with contempt, say, "You don't have the courage." I walked out of the room and back to where Joel sat in front of the blue tile oven in the living room. We both sat there quietly for perhaps ten minutes before Bodo appeared, stopped briefly to call out a somewhat loud good-bye, and went out the front door, slamming it behind him. The next morning I received a call from a hospital where Bodo had been brought in from the street, unconscious. "Will he live?" I asked. "Yes," the voice said, "he'll be all right. His stomach has been pumped out." I continued with my packing, when another call came: "Herr Uhse is asking for his son Joel." I do not remember what I answered, but I know I discouraged Joel from visiting him. It is a memory which continues to shame me. How often have I thought back on that scene with Bodo—it was the last time I was to see him—and how often have I asked myself, in wonder, How could I? Of course, I was in a heightened state of despair and fear, and I was reckless with rage, seeing Bodo as the cause of everything that was happening to me. Even so, looking back, I find no excuse for my harshness. Anyone is capable of crass inhumanity under certain circumstances, anything from causing a small hurt to committing serious crimes. There is always an explanation, but an excuse is harder to come up with—unless it is that we are human.

Once on the train at the Friedrichstrasse Station, we saw from the window some twenty-five friends waiting on the platform to see us off. They were party members mainly, and it was a kind of demonstration, an apparent effort to show their solidarity, sympathy, good wishes, whatever. But I especially remember Usch Gessner's distorted, crying face. I was her best friend. She didn't expect ever to see me again, just as I didn't expect ever to see her, or any of my friends, or the streets of the city where I had lived for twelve years.

We were scarcely two days out to sea on our way to New York when I realized I could eat again, and on the third day I was teaming up with Joel for the ship's Ping-Pong doubles tournament, which we won.

And so I recovered, physically at least, rather quickly. I was reminded of twenty years before, when I had, also with Joel, a baby, left New York by boat for Mexico. That was also in April, and I began to remember additional similarities: the dreadful year before I finally left, the same inability to eat and the loss of hair, Jim's suicide threat, and the pleas that I remain. The coincidence seemed strange to me.

One evening I dragged a deck chair as far as possible from where other people might congregate. I wanted to be alone, partly because it had begun to be a strain to parry the eternal question, where did I come from and where was I going? I lay bundled in one of the ship's blankets—the April night was chilly—feeling close to the sounds and smells around me: the faint hum of the ship's engine, distant voices, and the delicious sea air.

All my life, it seemed, I had felt the need to hide something about myself—sometimes that I was Jewish, often as a little girl, but also as an adult. And about my personal life and my various moves—from one country to another—always, it seemed, there was a need to be silent or not to tell all the truth: living with Jim unmarried, living with Bodo unmarried, Bodo a Communist. I needed to keep from my countrymen that I was living in East Germany, and on the ship, I had to try to be silent, certainly about my past. How could I speak, as everyone else seemed to, with apparent ease, of where I was going and why? America, I knew, was in a frenzy of anticommunism, and here was I, coming home from a life with Communists, with two children to support. I felt the trembling of the ship's engines carrying me farther and farther into the unknown, and I realized that, for perhaps the first time in my life, I was afraid of the future. A sense of adventure had always moved me forward, almost headlong, without much thought, unless it was the simple idea that it was better to move ahead than to remain. And I had always believed in myself and in something which would make everything come out all right.

I lay huddled in the soft wool blanket, listening to the faint voices and laughter coming from farther down the deck, and gazed out across the water. What would the future bring? I began mentally to list what I had: Joel, a sensitive, talented, healthy boy of twenty; Stefan, in Mexico. I hoped he would be cured when I got there, and I thought of how the United States, which he had never seen, might open up a new and better world for him. I thought of myself. I was almost forty-seven years old, but I had been down before and had come up again. I could count on a little money each month from Bodo, for a while anyway—dollars were in short supply in East Germany—and then, who knows, something would happen, I would find a way, something would get me through. I stopped thinking, realized I was sleepy, and walked down the deck and into my bunk.

Epilogue

It is almost three decades since my two sons and I left East Germany, and for the most recent fifteen of those years, my life has been very good. Someone recently asked me what the best years of my life have been, and I believe I startled my questioner by saying, quite truthfully, that for me they have been after sixty. Occasionally I have felt, and remarked, how grateful I am no longer to have to worry about the future, to make important decisions, or to think about what to do with my life, for I have already done it or it has been done to me—does it matter? Of course, I have been fortunate in having no health or money worries, and maybe I am fortunate too in wanting relatively little. That has resulted, strangely enough, in my having a good deal more than I need. For example, there are the unexpected royalty checks which come occasionally from overseas, from the continued sale of Bodo's books, and the weekend place which became mine, and a haven for whoever wishes, after the death of Bill, my third husband. Bill was six years younger than I. He died suddenly and unexpectedly, at age fifty-three, just five months after Stefan killed himself. That was in 1973.

The first few months after leaving East Germany were desperately lonely ones for me, and I found myself, at first, missing the very political atmosphere which I had previously thought I detested. Naturally I did not miss the dreadful year or so before leaving East Germany—and the departure itself, the uprooting, I remember as a kind of surgical operation without anesthesia. But when my thinking went back to the times before, I felt I had left a way of life that, at least in part, was superior to what I seemed to be going into. Now, after so many years, I no longer have that sense of having lost something that was valuable, but the memory is still there—a memory of a life of commonality and togetherness among the artists, writers, and professionals, and their wives and husbands. It was a kind of automatic drawing-together of people of like needs and interests, people with common purposes, dedicated to values and ideals larger than their own private concerns, so that each life was given meaning beyond an everyday blandness. I missed the intellectual atmosphere which I had become used to, and especially I missed listening to bright minds trying to find a solution for themselves, for Germany, and for the world.

On the other hand, it was a revelation finding myself in my own country after twenty years. I hadn't realized how much I missed simply speaking, and being around, my own language, and I was aware, almost immediately, of the relaxed atmosphere. I despised it at first, remembering the tension and high purpose of friends in East Germany, but I soon began to relax myself, and enjoy the pleasures of a return to New York. Even through my loneliness I was aware of and appreciated the brightness and immensity of New York City, the new buildings, the colors and variety of the cars, the traffic, the new one-way streets, and the gorgeous vegetable stands and supermarkets, with their staggering variety. In Berlin, there was mostly one of everything. Sometimes you had to stand in line, but then you took what you wanted or needed and went about your business. Here I can still find myself standing in a paroxysm of indecision before row upon row of breads and such—most of which, at least it seems to me, does not warrant the amount of time spent in the choosing. Naturally I was shocked, after East Germany, at the amount of simple waste—of food, things, and even lives. I was no longer used to squalor and poverty. I am not shocked anymore, however—just aware, like almost everyone else here, and doing my share of wasting too, as are those around me.

Some of the changes were surprising—new words, for instance, which were on everyone's lips as though they had always existed: words like *motel,* from *hotel* and *motor,* and *smog,* from *fog* and *smoke.* Nor did pizza or shopping malls exist before I left, nor that, to me, ugly, scraggly look of the outskirts of most middle-sized towns. But the change that most startled me was the sight of a young black girl behind a counter at Macy's department store. It was a sight unthinkable before I left the States, and to my shame, I don't remember having thought much about how Negroes supported themselves. They were in Harlem, in residential buildings that were not integrated. The women, when they were employed, worked farther downtown, usually in housework, and the men were mainly menials, with a small percentage of jazz musicians. It was unimaginable for a black face to appear on screen or stage except as a comic, a jazz player, or a servant, and never would one have seen a Negro behind a counter at Macy's. Want ads changed too, as I learned when I was searching for a job. No longer did potential employers specify, "Only Christians need apply," or, "No Jews." (To say, "No Negroes," had obviously been unnecessary.)

Such changes were, of course, no changes at all for Joel and Stefan, neither of them ever having spent any time in the States, except for Joel's first year of life.

I still don't know how I managed to get the three of us settled in our new life. Nor do I remember that the adjustment was that difficult. I found an apartment, Stefan got a scholarship at the private Walden School, and I soon got a job. It was my first job, and as it turned out, my last. The experience was, certainly at first, a needed lesson in humility. I was no longer the wife of an important and successful writer, and I had to take orders from impatient and indifferent young girls. Because of the political atmosphere, there was also the need, during the first year or so, of keeping my background secret. I had lied on my personnel forms, and no one knew of my twenty years outside the country, most of them in East Germany. So I had to do a good deal of bluffing, not knowing how to distinguish between what I was supposed to know and what was perhaps new to everyone around me. I believe I was more or less successful in keeping my ignorance from my co-workers, and even the reality that I had never worked in an office before, or ever used a stapler. I believe I had never even seen one. I was to remain there for eighteen years. Occasionally, during those years, someone who knew me and my background would remark that I didn't belong there. But I did, as much as anyone else who worked there, some to remain, some to go off to something else, better, worse, or simply different. I used to mind being asked, as one usually is at a social gathering, "What do you do?" Perhaps that is why I no longer ask that question of anyone else. I ask what the person is interested in, and I usually see a face brighten with the pleasure of telling about something cared about, occasionally something that happens to involve the workplace as well.

Stefan did more than well at the Walden School, since each report card contained accolades from his teachers, as well as from the school's principal, referring to his extraordinary intellect. I was proud of him, as the "best in the school," but also worried. He was becoming increasingly withdrawn and seemed to repulse all attempts, either mine or his peers', at any kind of closeness or understanding. He seemed without friends and, I thought, serious beyond his years.

I wasn't worried enough. I saw him as tall, slender, good-looking, immensely talented, disciplined, ambitious. I couldn't imagine anything getting in the way—I had only to wait and watch. I hadn't the slightest doubt that he was, or would become, one of the rarities of this world—a genius. It all seemed to be happening even sooner than I had expected when he wrote an antiwar play on Vietnam, directing it and acting in it himself, for his graduation from Walden. The performance received a long standing ovation, and later, an off-Broadway showing was highly praised in the *Village Voice*. He was seventeen, but was growing more and more reserved and so withdrawn that communication was becoming difficult. He did, however, accompany Joel some months afterward to Cuba, with a student group.

Watching him after he returned, I became seriously worried. There began the years of his search, and of my meager and eventually unsuccessful efforts to help him. Some time after Stefan's death, I wrote to a distant friend. I quote myself only because I believe I couldn't put it any clearer now, many years later:

Stefan's loneliness and suffering in Germany, both before and especially during the wrenching-apart of the family, was infinitely worse than Bodo's, mine, or Joel's. The thirteen years after that separation were spent mainly in a lonely search, first for answers to the whys of world troubles, and then, in a search for an answer for himself. He wrote steadily, he was always alone, he studied every possible aspect of life in great depth, all the philosophies and thought, from Marxism through to the organized religions, and possibly found some peace occasionally in Zen Buddhism (meditation). He was unable to communicate with anyone. All I could do was find the money or means for his journeys—searches—to India, Tibet, Japan, California, Pakistan, Turkey. He hated me—he loved me. I believe I was the only one who felt he was not completely crazy, though diagnosed a schizophrenic. He was finally hospitalized, after which he threw himself out of a window; then, after six months in a hospital all broken up, and then more or less mended, [he passed] another six months a cripple before the second, and successful,

throwing of himself out of his window at home. I have never stopped
mourning or wanting to understand the suffering and loneliness of his life.
He died on January 19, 1973.

Stefan's years of searching were single-minded, but I, like most people,
lived through those years on many levels. I began to sculpt, using a pamphlet
for beginners, and without other instruction made out of clay, and even
marble, figures and heads good enough to be accepted in a gallery and to
receive the praise I needed before I stopped sculpting, a year or so later. I also
met, around that time, my third husband, Bill Neuman. He was warm, gen-
erous, and loving. I married him for the emotional and social security he
could provide, but I think I also loved him. I became again used to having a
husband—I had not yet learned to be alone. For the most part, however, the
marriage was a mistake, since Bill wanted me, but not my problem. He was
incapable of understanding the seriousness of Stefan's troubles, or my own
drive to help him. So the years with Bill, with both of us working, were full
of conflict over Stefan—and torn as I was between the two, I invariably
moved in the direction of Stefan, who was clearly the more needing.

After Stefan's first suicide attempt, and during the six months he spent at
St. Vincent's Hospital, I went each day, after work, to sit with him, and the
six months afterward were mainly spent trying to find places for him, now a
cripple, to live. Doctors then—they have since changed their views on the
matter—believed that schizophrenics and their mothers should be kept apart.

Five months after Stefan dropped himself out of the high window of his
room, completing what he had attempted just a year before, Bill died suddenly. His death turned me about, somehow jolted me, and had the para-
doxical effect of easing some of the pain over Stefan's life and death.

I was sixty years old. Stefan's suffering was ended, Bill was dead, and I
soon began to notice that my own life was changing, almost imperceptibly at
first, then noticeably. I mark the change from just an hour before Stefan's
suicide. He was standing behind me in the hall of my apartment as I watched
his tall figure in the mirror before me. I did not give his gestures much importance at the time, but I have since become convinced that his movements and
words then, scarcely an hour before he was to die, had the power to change
my life. Simply put, it was a healing—a blessing: his hands moved up and
down near my body, hesitating and halting as they went from my head down

and up again, never touching, and all the while he spoke softly, saying, "You will be all right—I love you—I'm sorry if I've frightened you—you will benefit from the years you have helped me." And always his hands were moving and halting, up and down, some three inches from my body.

One of Stefan's studies was occult science, and as I have since learned, he was feeling the emanations from my body, sensing and touching the etheric field or aura around me.

Yoga and meditation became a way of life for me, and for some years I read only spiritual books. Perhaps it was the kind of reading I was doing, with the study and practice of yoga, perhaps it was Stefan's final blessing—at any rate, I slowly found myself in a very special state of being, although I was scarcely aware of it until much later. I am not going to try to describe it, because I know I am unable to. A sense of absolute fearlessness, peace, and freedom was part of it. It was in that state that I found myself, by the time I was sixty-two, loving another woman—a love as clear and uncluttered as my previous loves had been complicated and murky, hedged in as they were by need, social demands, and other complexities. I was relaxed in the knowledge that my love was returned, and I realized, in my new state, the golden truth that one receives all one could possibly require simply by not asking or wanting.

But I could not sustain that precious state of mind. Attachment and jealousy came in to mar what had seemed a perfect friendship. And yet, more and more, as the years pass, I am coming to realize the blessing of simply enjoying life as it comes to me, without worry or ambition, in the company of good friends.

Shortly before I was to retire, at age sixty-five, a young man telephoned to ask me to take part in a documentary he was preparing on the life of James Agee. The day before the filming, he visited me in my apartment to discuss what was involved. I told him I might have trouble remembering everything about Jim—so much time had gone by—and he suggested that I spend the hours until the following day trying to remember. "Just keep thinking Jim Agee," he said. I did, and the next day, when I returned from work, I found in the mail—by one of those inexplicable but meaningful coincidences—the letter from England, Jim's letter to me, written twenty-five years before, the letter which set me to writing this story about myself.